THE
COMMUNION
OF SAINTS

THE
COMMUNION
OF SAINTS

Living in Fellowship with the People of God

Edited by

PHILIP GRAHAM RYKEN

P U B L I S H I N G

P.O. BOX 817 • PHILLIPSBURG • NEW JERSEY 08865-0817

Page design by Tobias Design
Typesetting by Michelle Feaster

Printed in the United States of America

ISBN-10: 0-87552-507-5
ISBN-13: 978-0-87552-507-5

Contents

Preface

Americans have started bowling alone. Back in the 1960s and 1970s, bowling was among the nation's most popular team sports, with almost 10 percent of Americans participating in a bowling league. This may not seem significant, especially to nonbowlers; however, Harvard professor Robert Putnam thinks it symbolizes an important shift in American culture. In a book entitled *Bowling Alone*, Putnam shows that by almost every measure, participation in civic life is at a record low. Socially and politically, Americans are less connected than ever.[1]

Even church attendance is down, having declined by as much as 10 percent in recent decades. And those who do attend seem to have less and less time to commit to their congregation's worship and ministry. Church has become a place we go rather than a community to which we belong. Yet the truth is that there is no such thing as private Christianity—Christianity without the active communion of the saints. As Charles Colson has argued,

> Christians who understand their personal identity as followers of Christ will not make a widespread difference in the decline and decay around us—unless we have a high view of our corporate identity as the body of Christ. . . . Christianity is not a solitary belief system. Any genuine resurgence of Christianity, as history demonstrates, depends on a reawakening and re-

newal of that which is the essence of the faith—that is, the people of God, the new society, the body of Christ, which is made manifest in the world—the Church.[2]

A privatized faith weakens the church within and without, loosening the bonds of true Christian community and hindering the church's witness to the world.

It was a concern for the corporate life of Christ's body that led a small group of pastors and teachers to plan an adult Bible school class called "The Communion of Saints." The class, which ran for thirteen weeks at Tenth Presbyterian Church in Philadelphia, was designed to strengthen Christian fellowship in the local church. To establish a proper biblical and theological foundation, the course was organized around chapter 26 in the Westminster Confession of Faith. It was also designed to be practical, with most class sessions including time for asking questions, making comments, offering suggestions, and praying for God to strengthen the communion of the saints at Tenth Presbyterian Church.

These class sessions also formed the basis for the present book, which from the beginning has been a group effort—a practical exercise in the communion of saints. Eight people did most of the writing: Dr. Hughes Oliphant Old from Princeton's Center for Theological Inquiry wrote "Baptized into Communion" (chap. 3) and "Assembly Required" (chap. 6). The Reverend D. Marion Clark, who now serves as senior pastor of First Presbyterian Church in Gainesville, Florida, wrote "Members Only" (chap. 4). Dr. William Edgar, who is professor of apologetics at Westminster Theological Seminary in Philadelphia, contributed "United in Love" (chap. 5). The chapters on "The Communion Table" (7) and "Gifts and Graces" (8) were written by the Honorable Thomas Martin, a judge in Chester County, Pennsylvania. Dr. George McFarland, chairman of the history department and vice-principal of the high school at Delaware County Christian Schools, contributed "Relief in Outward Things" (chap. 9) and "Mutual Edification" (chap. 10). And the Reverend Howard Blair, a semi-retired missionary to Japan, wrote on "Worldwide Communion" (chap. 12). I wrote the remaining four chapters, and Lydia Brown-back, media manager for the Alliance of Confessing Evangelicals, prepared the leader's guide.

Once a complete draft of the manuscript and study materials was available, it was previewed by Bible studies meeting in the homes of John and Chris Felser and David and Susan Madder. Members of these small groups critiqued each chapter, carefully noting ideas that needed amplification or clarification. Finally, as I prepared the manuscript for publication, each contributor had a final opportunity to review and revise it.

As we worked together on this project, we learned from one another, benefiting from the unique gifts and special insights of each participant. In the process, we came to have a deeper appreciation for the communion that we share in Christ. We understand what Dietrich Bonhoeffer meant when he wrote, "Let him who until now has had the privilege of living a common Christian life with other Christians praise God's grace from the bottom of his heart. Let him thank God on his knees and declare: It is grace, nothing but grace, that we are allowed to live in community with Christian brethren."[3] It is our prayer that everyone who reads this book will learn to offer the same prayer and will "have power, *together with all the saints*, to grasp how wide and long and high and deep is the love of Christ" (Eph. 3:18).

Proceeds from the sale of this book go to China Ministries International for the translation and distribution of Reformed literature in the Chinese world. This too is an expression of our communion as saints—a small gift offered in the certain hope that one day we will all gather to worship God in his glory.

PHILIP GRAHAM RYKEN
PHILADELPHIA

ONE

What Is the Communion of Saints?

I pray that you, being rooted and established in love, may have power, together with all the saints, to grasp how wide and long and high and deep is the love of Christ. (Eph. 3:17b–18)

I believe in the communion of saints. (The Apostles' Creed)

In 1630 the devout Puritan governor of the Massachusetts Bay Company led a small group of colonists to the shores of North America. His name was John Winthrop (1588–1649), and as his ship, the *Arbella*, sailed the Atlantic, the governor stood on the deck and charged his followers to establish a new kind of Christian community:

> We must be knit together in this work as one man, we must entertain each other in brotherly affection . . . , we must uphold a familiar commerce together in all meekness, gentleness, patience and liberality, we must delight in each other, make others' conditions our own, rejoice together, mourn together, labor and suffer together, always having before our

eyes our commission and community in the work, our community as members of the same body, so shall we keep the
unity of the spirit in the bond of peace, the Lord will be our
God and delight to dwell among us.[1]

What Winthrop proposed was a living fellowship of love centered in
Jesus Christ. The community he envisioned would be animated by
the sanctifying work of the Holy Spirit, who would enable the people
who lived in it to share a common life of unity, charity, and generosity. To put this idea in its simplest terms, Winthrop believed in the
communion of saints.

"I Believe in the Communion of Saints"

John Winthrop was not alone. Most Christians believe in the
communion of saints . . . or at least they say that they do. Anyone who
has ever recited the Apostles' Creed has said it before: "I believe in the
communion of saints." Depending on the order of worship in their
churches, some Christians make this confession hundreds or even
thousands of times. But many are unsure what it means. What is the
communion of saints?

The phrase "I believe in the communion of saints" was a late addition to the Apostles' Creed. The creed seems to have been formu-
lated sometime during the second century of the Christian era. But
Irenaeus in the second century, Tertullian in the third century, and
Rufinus in the fourth century did not confess a belief in the communion of the saints, at least in so many words. Even as late as A.D. 400,
Augustine's commentary on the Apostles' Creed made no mention of
the communion of the saints.[2]

As far as we know, the first reference to the "communion of saints"
(or *communio sanctorum*) appears in a sermon by Nicetas of Reme-

siana, who died early in the fifth century. However, by A.D. 550 the phrase had become an established part of the Apostles' Creed. Christians were not content to believe in "the holy catholic church." They also wanted to confess "the communion of saints."

The communion of the saints is not simply the blessed community that the saints enjoy in heaven. Nor does it involve personal communication between the living and the dead, which is how some of the earliest commentators seem to have understood it. This is also how the Roman Catholic Church and many Eastern Orthodox leaders understand the communion of saints to the present day. This misunderstanding started with the recognition that some Christians live exemplary lives. After death these Christians, especially those who had been martyred for their faith, were revered for their godliness. In time holy men and women came to be venerated, and their personal belongings were treated as holy relics. Furthermore, since they were already in heaven, it seemed reasonable to think that they had special access to God. Thus some people started praying to the glorified saints instead of praying to God. Eventually this so-called communion of saints became a substitute for communion with God.[3] Of course it is good to learn from the heroes and heroines of the faith. But it is wrong to worship them, venerate them, pray to them, or in any way consider them mediators between humanity and God.

Another misunderstanding is to assume that the communion of the saints is exactly the same thing as the church. For example, Martin Luther (1483–1546) taught that the "the holy Christian church" and "the communion of the saints" were identical. For Luther, the communion of the saints was "nothing but a comment or interpretation by which someone wished to explain what the Christian church is."[4] One problem with Luther's view is that it makes the Apostles' Creed redundant. If the church and the communion of the saints are identical, then the Apostles' Creed merely repeats itself when the words "I believe in the holy, catholic church" are followed by the words "I believe in the communion of saints." Thus we are led to conclude that although the holy, catholic church is one place where the saints enjoy their happy communion, the two are not identical. So what is the difference?

One difference is that the communion of saints includes believers who are in heaven, whereas the church is limited to those who remain on earth. True, some theologians distinguish between the church militant, which wages spiritual warfare on earth, and the church triumphant, which has entered into glory. But while the New Testament generally reserves the term *church (ekklesia)* for the earthly gathering of God's elect (e.g., 1 Cor. 1:2; Gal. 1:2), the communion of saints extends beyond the church to embrace the company of heaven. Without falling into the error of worshiping the saints in glory, we nevertheless are joined to them through faith in Jesus Christ. This connection is expressed in a beautiful stanza from William Walsham How's hymn "For All the Saints":

> Oh, bless'd communion, fellowship divine!
> We feebly struggle, they in glory shine,
> Yet all are one in thee, for all are thine.
> Alleluia! Alleluia!

The dead are dead in Christ and the living are alive in Christ, so all the saints are connected to Christ. This book will focus primarily on our communion with the saints on earth. This is because at present there are some aspects of fellowship that we cannot share with the saints in glory. But when Christ returns, he will gather us all together to enjoy complete communion.

Another difference between the communion of saints and the holy, catholic church is that this communion will outlast the church. The visible church is a temporary institution. Although the people of

God will live for all eternity, many aspects of the visible church will disappear when Christ returns to establish his kingdom. Presumably there will be no evangelists, no sacraments, and no church discipline in heaven. In the words of the Westminster Confession of Faith, "the ministry, oracles, and ordinances of God, for the gathering and perfecting of the saints, in this life" will last only until "the end of the world" (25.3). But the communion of saints will last forever, as God's people enjoy everlasting fellowship with the triune God and with one another. In the meantime, the church helps to promote and preserve the communion of saints. James Bannerman wrote:

> According to the arrangement of God, the Christian is more of a Christian in society than alone, and more in the enjoyment of privileges of a spiritual kind when he shares them with others, than when he possesses them apart. . . . The Christian Church was established in the world, to realize the superior advantages of a social over an individual Christianity, and to set up and maintain the communion of the saints.[5]

The communion of saints is one aspect of what is sometimes called the *invisible church*. The invisible church is "the whole number of the elect, that have been, are, or shall be gathered into one, under Christ the Head" (Confession of Faith, 25.1). In other words, the invisible church consists of all true believers, and not just those who say that they are Christians. The members of this invisible church have fellowship or communion with one another. As the apostle Paul reminded the Christians in Rome, "in Christ we who are many form one body, and each member belongs to all the others" (Rom. 12:5). The communion of saints is the common spiritual life that is shared by every member of the invisible church.

5

Who the Saints Are

In order to understand the communion of saints it is necessary to know what is meant by the word *saint*. The first thing to point out is that a saint does not belong to a special category of believers. Sainthood is not a lifetime achievement award for martyrs, evangelists, and prayer warriors. Saints are not members of a spiritual Hall of Fame. Rather, a saint is nothing more and nothing less than an ordinary Christian. This is why it was customary in New Testament times and long afterwards for Christians to call one another "saints," no matter how unspiritual they may have seemed. The apostle Paul followed this practice by greeting Christians as "saints" in many of his letters. "To the saints in Ephesus," he would write (Eph. 1:1), or "Greet all the saints in Christ Jesus" (Phil. 4:21).

There is something curious about the biblical use of the word *saint* that helps to show that saints are regular Christians. Although the various words for "saint" occur hundreds of times in the Bible, they almost never occur in the singular. The Bible speaks of "the saints" but not "a saint." The singular thing about saints, therefore, is that they are always found in the plural. Saints are never found here and there, somewhere off by themselves. They are found wherever there are Christians, because every believer is a saint. Thus anyone who knows Christ is included in the communion of saints.

Literally, the "saints" are the "holy ones." They are holy for three reasons. First, they are declared holy in their *justification*. They are not holy by virtue of their virtues. In fact, there is a sense in which the communion of saints is a communion of sinners. But these sinners have been made holy on the basis of the righteousness of Jesus Christ. Christ has become their "righteousness, holiness and redemption" (1 Cor. 1:30). They do not stand before God on the basis of their own holiness. Rather, they "have been made holy through the sacrifice of the body of Jesus Christ once for all" (Heb. 10:10). Saints are sinners justified by grace.

Second, the saints are made holy in their _sanctification_. On the basis of their justification, believers are considered saints from the moment that they put their trust in Christ. At the same time, they experience a spiritual transformation that gives them a new capacity for holiness, and they continue to become more holy all the time. They are "sanctified in Christ Jesus and called to be holy" (1 Cor. 1:2; cf. 1 Thess. 3:7). First the saints are declared holy; then they are made holy as the Holy Spirit enables them to forsake sin and to follow Christ in new obedience. Sanctification is something like spiritual boot camp. It takes more than enlisting in the army to prepare someone for battle. Boot camp transforms a civilian into a soldier. Similarly it takes more than conversion to train someone to live a holy life. Sanctification transforms a sinner into a saint.

Third, the saints are identified as holy by their _separation_. To be holy is to be separated from what is profane. Old Testament believers were set apart from the world by being circumcised, keeping the Sabbath, refraining from unclean foods, and maintaining proper worship in the temple. Their need to be separate from the world was expressed by the prophet Isaiah: "Depart, depart, go out from there! Touch no unclean thing! Come out from it and be pure" (Isa. 52:11). The New Testament saints are holy in the same way. Although they are in the world, "they are not of the world" (John 17:14), for Christ calls them to separate themselves from worldly words, attitudes, and actions. The Christian community is a holy community.

The late German Reformer Zacharias Ursinus (1534–83) summarized the biblical teaching about sainthood: "Believers are called _saints_ in three respects: by the imputation of Christ's righteousness; by the beginning of conformity to the law which is commenced in them; and by their separation from the rest of the human race, being called of God to the end that they may truly know and worship him."[6] To put this in simple theological terms, the saints are holy because of their justification, sanctification, and separation.

What Communion Is

Now that we know who the saints are, the next question to ask is What is meant by communion? To have communion is to share something in common. The German Reformed theologian Johan Heidegger thus defined the communion of saints as "the union, society and assembly of all believers who have something in common with each other."[7] So the question becomes What do the saints share in common?

The answer is that the saints share almost everything in common—at least everything that matters. Because they are joined by the common fact of their salvation in Jesus Christ, they have an equal share in all his benefits. In their common life as a new community in Christ, they share the spiritual gifts that equip them for their common work in the gospel. The basis for their communion is expressed perhaps most powerfully in Paul's letter to the Ephesians: "Make every effort to keep the unity of the Spirit through the bond of peace. There is one body and one Spirit—just as you were called to one hope when you were called—one Lord, one faith, one baptism; one God and Father of all, who is over all and through all and in all" (Eph. 4:3–6). In these verses Paul describes the Christian community as a common body, connected by a common Spirit, entered by a common calling, destined for a common glory, serving a common Lord, on the basis of a common faith, sealed by a common sacrament (baptism), to the glory of a common God, who is the Father of all.

Perhaps this is the best place to define the communion of saints. The doctrine is so rich and deep that it defies a simple explanation, but one of the best and fullest definitions comes from chapter 26 of the Westminster Confession of Faith:

I. All saints, that are united to Jesus Christ their Head, by His Spirit, and by faith, have fellowship with Him in His grace, sufferings, death, resurrection, and glory: and, being united to

8

one another in love, they have communion in each other's gifts and graces, and are obliged to the performance of such duties, public and private, as do conduce to their mutual good, both in the inward and outward man.

II. Saints by profession are bound to maintain an holy fellowship and communion in the worship of God, and in performing such other spiritual services as tend to their mutual edification; as also in relieving each other in outward things, according to their several abilities and necessities. Which communion, as God offereth opportunity, is to be extended unto all those who, in every place, call upon the name of the Lord Jesus.

III. This communion which the saints have with Christ, doth not make them in any wise partakers of the substance of His Godhead; or to be equal with Christ in any respect: either of which to affirm is impious and blasphemous. Nor doth their communion one with another, as saints, take away, or infringe the title or propriety which each man hath in his goods and possessions.

Shorter definitions are possible. Luther described the communion of the saints as "a community of pure saints . . . called together by the Holy Spirit in one faith, mind, and understanding."[8] Ursinus understood the doctrine of the communion of saints to mean "first, that all and every one who believes, being members of Christ, are in common partakers of him, and of all his riches and gifts; secondly, that every one must know it to be his duty, readily and cheerfully to employ his gifts for the advantage and salvation of other members."[9] Here is another definition: *The communion of saints is the living fellowship of all true believers who are united in love by their union with*

9

Christ and have spiritual communion with one another as they share in corporate worship, spiritual gifts, Christian graces, material goods, and mutual edification. The rest of this book is about how to practice and promote this godly communion.✝

Divided We Fall

It is not easy to practice the communion of saints. The isolation of the saints is as old as the fall. The sin of Adam and Eve made a breach in their communion with one another as well as with God. In his legal defense Adam managed to attack the woman as well as the Creator: "The woman you put here with me—she gave me some fruit from the tree, and I ate it" (Gen. 3:12). Sin brought anger, shame, alienation, and recrimination into human relationships. As Dietrich Bonhoeffer (1906–45) pointed out in his definitive work on the communion of the saints, "medieval symbolism for the Fall puts a tree in the center, with the serpent coiled round it, and on either side the man and the woman, separated by the tree from which they disobediently ate."[10]

The sins of others often disturb the communion of the saints. James Montgomery Boice (1938–2000) used to tell the story about the Scotsman who doodled during a sermon. The man wrote a short poem that was discovered in one of the pews after the service. He seems to have been looking around at his fellow worshipers, for he wrote,

> To dwell above with saints in love,
>   Aye, that will be glory!
> To dwell below with saints I know,
>   Now that's a different story.[11]

Most Christians have read a few chapters of that "different story" and in doing so have discovered that most saints are not very saintly after all. Most—possibly all—sins disrupt the communion of the saints. This is true of obvious sins like lying, stealing, murder, and adultery. But it is also true of private sins like greed, selfishness, gossip, and slander. As cartoonist Walt Kelly's Pogo said, "We have met the enemy, and he is us."

Another obstacle to the communion of the saints is the pride of individualism. This is especially a problem in the American church. When the French statesman Alexis de Tocqueville (1805–59) visited the United States in the 1830s he observed that Americans "owe nothing to any man, they expect nothing from any man, they acquire the habit of always considering themselves as standing alone, and they are apt to imagine that their whole destiny is in their hands. . . . [This attitude] throws [the American] back forever upon himself alone, and threatens in the end to confine him entirely within the solitude of his own heart."[12]

The pride of individualism has infected the American church. Thomas Jefferson liked to observe, "I am a sect myself." Thomas Paine said, "My mind is my church." Now many Americans are raising Paine in the contemporary church. They doubt the necessity of active involvement in a living church. They rely on Christian radio, worship at home with a televangelist, or treat churches like leased automobiles, trading the old one in for a new one every five years.

The saints are also divided by class, ethnicity, and gender. These differences are part of God's providence in creation, and as we shall see in chapter 11, the way that the saints complement one another adds to the beauty of their communion. But when social, racial, and sexual distinctions are corrupted by sin, they become obstacles to Christian fellowship. The communion of saints is disturbed whenever race becomes a pretext for racism, class becomes a pretext for classism, or sex becomes a pretext for sexism. Identifying these sins as sins is not a matter of being politically correct but biblically correct (see Gal. 3:28).

Another obstacle to the communion of the saints is schism. In the words of the old hymn, the church is "by schisms rent asunder." Some denominational distinctives are necessary to preserve the purity of the church, but such divisions are often the sad result of moral or doctrinal error. The existence of different denominations represents a failure of saintly communion.

Finally, the saints are separated by time and space. Although Christian books enable the faith of the past to live in the present, individual Christians cannot engage in heart-to-heart spiritual communion across the centuries. Even geography hinders the communion of saints: Because we are scattered across the globe we cannot meet for common worship.

The sad result of these many obstacles is the isolation of the saints. We are divided rather than united. We are like the characters in Maurice Maeterlinck's (1862–1949) haunting play, *The Sightless*, which depicts twelve blind people lost in a forest. The message of Maeterlinck's play is expressed in these words from the oldest blind man: *"We have never seen each other; we question each other, and we answer each other, we live together and we are always together, but we know not what we are. For years and years we have lived together and we have never *beheld* each other. One would say we are always alone."* The same might well be said of the church, that although we are always meeting together, we are often alone.

Somehow we know that what God said to Adam is true for us all: "It is not good for the man to be alone" (Gen. 2:18a). Deep down we desire the kind of intimate fellowship described in the New Testament. We long to make a spiritual connection with all the saints, living to love others rather than ourselves. So we continue to say that we believe in the communion of the saints.

The question is Do we practice this communion? To employ the language of the Westminster Confession, Are we "united to one another in love"? Do we "share in one another's gifts and graces"? Do we "maintain holy fellowship in the worship of God"? Do we "relieve each other in outward things"? Do we "perform such spiritual services as tend to our mutual edification"? And do we "extend this communion to all those in every place who call upon the name of the Lord Jesus"? The sad truth is that most Christians in most churches do not do most of these things as often or as well as they ought to be done. The purpose of this book is to help us rediscover the lost communion of the saints.

Union with Christ

Praise be to the God and Father of our Lord Jesus Christ,
who has blessed us in the heavenly realms with every spiritual
blessing in Christ. (Eph. 1:3)

All saints, that are united to Jesus Christ their Head, by His Spirit,
and by faith, have fellowship with Him in His grace, sufferings, death,
resurrection, and glory. (Westminster Confession of Faith, 26.1)

Where there is no union there can be no communion. In fact, the word *communion* cannot even be spelled without "union." In order for people to have communion with one another they must be connected by some common bond. For example, motorcycle enthusiasts are united by their love for Harley-Davidsons. Basketball players are united by the uniforms they wear. The Teamsters are united by the labor they perform. Family members are united by flesh and blood. The United States are united by a common constitution. Some form of union provides the basis for every communion. There is no communion without union.

The same is true for the communion of the saints: *There is no communion of saints apart from union with Christ*. In chapter 1 we noted that Johan Heidegger defined the communion of saints as "the union, society and assembly of all believers who have something in common with each other." Heidegger went on to explain precisely what the saints share in common: "Now this common thing is Christ the Head of the Church, as well as the gifts which flow down from Him as Head to the Body."[1] The saints have communion with one another because together they participate in Christ and all his benefits.

The apostle John loved the communion of the saints. The reason that he wrote his first epistle was to promote such communion: "We proclaim to you what we have seen and heard so that you also may have fellowship with us" (1 John 1:3a). What connection provides the basis for this communion? Union with Christ: "Our fellowship is with the Father and with his Son, Jesus Christ" (1 John 1:3b). Fellowship with other believers comes from having fellowship with God through Jesus Christ. Communion is not something that we can create (although it is something that we must maintain) but something that we receive as a gift of salvation. Our communion as saints flows from our union with Christ, to whom we are joined by the Holy Spirit. As John MacArthur has written, "Anybody in fellowship with Jesus Christ is also in fellowship with anybody else in fellowship with Jesus Christ. This is our common ground. It is not social, economic, intellectual, cosmetic, or anything else superficial. Our common ground is that which is pulsing through the life of every Christian—the heartbeat of God."[2]

A Matter of Life and Death

"In Christ." It is such a little phrase that it is easy to read right past it, but the Bible uses these two words to express the powerful reality of the union between Christ and the Christian. Once one starts to notice it, that union seems to show up on every page of the New Testament.

Often believers are said to be in Christ: "If anyone is in Christ, he is a new creation" (2 Cor. 5:17). The epistle to the Philippians is addressed "to all the saints in Christ Jesus at Philippi" (Phil. 1:1). The reason that the saints can be addressed this way is because they find their identity in Christ: "There is neither Jew nor Greek, slave nor free, male nor female, for you are all one in Christ Jesus" (Gal. 3:28). On other occasions the Bible speaks of Jesus Christ in the believer: "I have been crucified with Christ and I no longer live, but Christ lives in me" (Gal. 2:20). Paul wrote to the Colossians about the glorious mystery "that has been kept hidden for ages and generations, but is now disclosed to the saints" (Col. 1:26). What is this mystery? It is "Christ in you, the hope of glory" (Col. 1:27).

Christ is in us, and we are in Christ. The two sides of this relationship sometimes appear together in Scripture. Jesus told his disciples, "Remain in me, and I will remain in you" (John 15:4). The apostle John described union with Christ as a mutual indwelling: "We know that we live in him and he in us, because he has given us of his Spirit" (1 John 4:13). Union with Christ is a mutual relationship. It can be compared with a fishing vessel that takes to the high seas. Once it leaves the harbor the boat is in the ocean. If the boat has a holding tank to keep its catch fresh, then the ocean is also in the boat. In a similar way, we are in Christ, and Christ is in us.

The reason that the New Testament speaks again and again about being in Christ is that union with Christ is the fundamental reality of the Christian life. Professor John Murray (1898–1975) observed that union with Christ "is not simply a step in the application of redemption . . . it underlies every step of the application of redemption. Union with Christ is really the central truth of the whole doctrine of salvation."[3] Therefore union with Christ is not just for super-Christians. It is not something that is only for believers who lead Bible studies, do door-to-door evangelism, and attend evening church. Rather, union with Christ is what it means to be a Christian. Anyone who is not in Christ is not a Christian. John Calvin (1509–64) explained the necessity of union with Christ in the strongest terms: "We must understand that as long as Christ remains outside of us, and we are separated from him, all that he has suffered and done for the salvation of the human race remains useless and of no value for us. . . . All that he possesses is nothing to us until we grow into one body with him."[4]

If we are not united to Christ, then we do not have access to any of his benefits. If we are not in Christ, then we have no part in his death on the cross to atone for sins. Nor do we have a share in his resurrection from the dead. We are not saved until we have been made one with Christ. Union with Christ is a matter of spiritual life and death.

Union Initiated

What if we *are* united to Christ? What then? If we are united to Jesus Christ then everything he has done for our salvation belongs to us. Everything Christ has to offer becomes ours when we are united to him. "In him [Christ] you have been enriched in every way" (1 Cor. 1:5); "Praise be to the God and Father of our Lord Jesus Christ, who has blessed us in the heavenly realms with every spiritual blessing in Christ" (Eph. 1:3). Whatever spiritual blessing we may care to mention, it comes through union and communion with Jesus Christ. Sinclair Ferguson writes, "Union with Christ is the foundation of all our spiritual experience and all spiritual blessings."[5]

To begin at the beginning, *election* is in union with Christ. As Paul goes on to explain to the Ephesians, "He [God] chose us in him [Christ] before the creation of the world" (Eph. 1:4). This is the electing grace of God. God's decision to unite us to Christ was made in eternity past, even before the creation of the world. Union with Christ goes back as far as God himself.

This mysterious electing decree becomes a personal spiritual re-

ality when we are united with Christ in our *regeneration*: "God, who
is rich in mercy, made us alive with Christ even when we were dead
in transgressions" (Eph. 2:4–5). The transition from spiritual death to
spiritual life—that is to say, the new birth or regeneration of the believer—happens with Christ. We become Christians when God calls
us "into fellowship with his Son Jesus Christ our Lord" (1 Cor. 1:9).
To put this another way, we are created in Christ Jesus in our regeneration (Eph. 1:10).

The same is true of *justification*. Justification is the declaration by
which God imputes or credits the righteousness of Christ to the believer. How does it happen? It happens in Christ: "God made him
[Christ] who had no sin to be sin for us, so that in him we might become the righteousness of God" (2 Cor. 5:21); "You are in Christ Jesus, who has become for us wisdom from God—that is, our
righteousness, holiness and redemption" (1 Cor. 1:30). The believer
is declared righteous by virtue of union with Christ. The reason that
the apostle Paul desired to "gain Christ and be found in him" was because he wanted to be justified. He was not content "having a righteousness of [his] own that comes from the law"; he wanted that which
is "through faith in Christ" (Phil. 3:9).

This verse reminds us that we receive the blessings of union with
Christ by faith. The New Testament speaks of trusting in or believing
in Jesus Christ dozens of times. For example, when Jesus performed
his first miracle at Cana, "his disciples put their faith in him" (John
2:11). Anyone who wants to be united to Christ must believe in him,
"so that Christ may dwell in your heart through faith" (Eph. 3:17).

Although union with Christ is by faith, faith is not the only bond
that unites us to Christ. At the same time that we unite ourselves to
Christ by faith, Christ unites himself to us by his Holy Spirit: "If anyone does not have the Spirit of Christ, he does not belong to Christ"
(Rom. 8:9b), but "he who unites himself with the Lord is one with
him in Spirit" (1 Cor. 6:17). "We know that we live in him and he in

us, because he has given us of his Spirit" (1 John 4:13; cf. John 14:16–17). The Puritans thus spoke of faith and the Holy Spirit as the "double bond" that unites Christ and the Christian. In the words of Obadiah Sedgwick (1600?–1658), "as faith makes up the union from us to Christ . . . so the Spirit makes the union 'twixt Christ and us."[6]

What about *sanctification*? Sanctification is the process by which a sinner becomes saintly. To put it another way, it is the process by which the Holy Spirit makes us more and more like Christ. Such progress in holiness is the supernatural result of being united to Christ, "for we are God's workmanship, created in Christ Jesus to do good works" (Eph. 2:10). Jesus taught his disciples that becoming sanctified depends on remaining connected to him: "No branch can bear fruit by itself; it must remain in the vine. Neither can you bear fruit unless you remain in me. I am the vine; you are the branches. If a man remains in me and I in him, he will bear much fruit; apart from me you can do nothing" (John 15:4–5). If we are united to Christ, then we will have abundant growth in grace. If not, we will not grow.

Union Perpetuated

Perseverance is also by union with Christ. Those who have been truly united to Christ can never be separated from him. This doctrine is called "the perseverance of the saints." Jesus declared that once he has taken hold of his sheep, "they shall never perish; no one can snatch them out of my hand" (John 10:28). We do not persevere with Christ in the strength of our faith. Rather, it is Christ who perseveres with us, for nothing is "able to separate us from the love of God that is in Christ Jesus our Lord" (Rom. 8:39b).

The perseverance of the saints depends on the double bond of union with Christ: faith and the Holy Spirit. The Scottish theologian

Thomas Boston (1676–1732) offered a beautiful illustration of the security this double bond provides:

> Were it so that the believer only apprehended Christ, but Christ apprehended not him, we could promise little as to the stability of such a union, it might quickly be dissolved; but as the believer apprehends Christ by faith, so Christ apprehends him by His Spirit, and none shall pluck him out of His hand. Did the child only keep hold of the nurse, it might at length grow weary, and let go its hold, and so fall away: but if she have her arms about the child, it is in no hazard of falling away, even though it be not actually holding by her. So, whatever sinful intermissions may happen in the exercise of faith, yet the union remains sure, by reason of the constant indwelling of the Spirit.[7]

Not even death brings union with Christ to an end. Believers die in Christ (Rev. 14:13) and they are "dead in Christ" (1 Thess. 4:16). Truly, for the Christian, union with Christ is a matter of life *and* death. We are united to Christ in death as well as life: "If we live, we live to the Lord; and if we die, we die to the Lord. So, whether we live or die, we belong to the Lord" (Rom. 14:8). This truth is vividly expressed in the Westminster Shorter Catechism, which asks, "What benefits do believers receive from Christ at death?" The answer is, "The souls of believers are at their death made perfect in holiness, and do immediately pass into glory; and their bodies, *being still united to Christ*, do rest in their graves till the resurrection" (Q. & A. 37, emphasis added). Even in their graves, the bodies of deceased believers remain united to Christ. And if death is in union with Christ, so is life after death. The resurrection of the body will be resurrection in union with Christ: "As in Adam all die, so in Christ all will be made alive" (1 Cor. 15:22). Every believer will receive resurrection life in and through Jesus Christ, for "if we died with Christ, we believe that we will also live with him" (Rom. 6:8).

Finally, *glorification* will occur through our union with Christ. Glorification is the permanent, instantaneous transformation of the believer into the glorious image of Jesus Christ. This glorious change will take place in the closest possible connection with Jesus Christ. "When Christ, who is your life, appears, then you also will appear with him in glory" (Col. 3:4). Just as we now share in the sufferings of Christ, so then "we may also share in his glory" (Rom. 8:17). Thus the end of all our ends and the glory of all our glories will take place in union with Christ. "Future glory will be nothing other than a continued unfolding of the riches of union with Christ."[8]

From eternity to eternity we are united to Christ: election-regeneration-justification-sanctification-perseverance-resurrection-glorification. In the words of Murray, union with Christ "embraces the wide span of salvation from its ultimate source in the eternal election of God to its final fruition in the glorification of the elect."[9] Without beginning and without end, every aspect of our salvation is wrapped up in our union with Jesus Christ. This does not mean that the saints become so absorbed into Christ as to lose their personal identity. "This communion which the saints have with Christ" does not make them "partakers of the substance of His Godhead" or "equal with Christ in any respect" (Confession of Faith, 26.3). When the saints are united to Christ they do not become Christs. However, they do become like Christ—and gloriously so!

Union Illustrated

What is it like to be united to Christ? To explain this mystery, the Bible gives vivid pictures of union with Christ, each of which emphasizes a different aspect of that union.

Jesus taught his disciples that being united to him is like being a branch in a vine:

> I am the vine; you are the branches. If a man remains in me and I in him, he will bear much fruit; apart from me you can do nothing. If anyone does not remain in me, he is like a branch that is thrown away and withers; such branches are picked up, thrown into the fire and burned. If you remain in me and my words remain in you, ask whatever you wish, and it will be given you. This is to my Father's glory, that you bear much fruit, showing yourselves to be my disciples. (John 15:5–8)

The picture of the vine and branches teaches that a relationship with Jesus Christ is a life-giving relationship. The Christian lives in Christ, the source of all vitality. If we are not connected to Christ, we will not bear fruit. Instead, we will be pruned from the vine, for union with Christ is a matter of life or death. But if we do know Christ, then his life flows into our lives and we will become fruitful disciples.

Being united to Christ can also be compared with being part of a body. As the apostle Paul explained, "The body is a unit, though it is made up of many parts; and though all its parts are many, they form one body. So it is with Christ. For we were all baptized by one Spirit into one body" (1 Cor. 12:12–13). Being united to Christ is like being united to a body. As the Scripture goes on to say, "You are the body of Christ, and each one of you is a part of it" (1 Cor. 12:27).

The body is one of Paul's favorite pictures of union with Christ. He speaks of suffering "for the sake of his [Christ's] body, which is the church" (Col. 1:24). "In Christ"—there are those two little words again—"we who are many form one body" (Rom. 12:5); "We are all members of one body" (Eph. 4:25; cf. 5:30). This truth is so basic that Paul seemingly gets exasperated when the Corinthians need to have it explained to them again: "Do you not know that your bodies are members of Christ himself?" (1 Cor. 6:15).

Like the picture of the vine and branches, the picture of the body shows that union with Christ is a vital, living relationship. It also teaches us something about the role that Christ has in that relationship. If being united to Christ is like being part of a body, then Christ is the head who governs and directs the body: "Christ is the head of the church, his body, of which he is the Savior" (Eph. 5:23).

Union with Christ can also be compared with a marriage, like the one described in Ephesians 5, where Paul quotes Genesis 2:24: "For this reason a man will leave his father and mother and be united to his wife, and the two will become one flesh" (Eph. 5:31). Although this verse seems to be about human marriage, the apostle is also addressing spiritual matrimony: "This is a profound mystery—but I am talking about Christ and the church" (Eph. 5:32). The union of Christ and the Christian is like the covenantal, spiritual, emotional, and physical union between a husband and a wife.

The marriage between God and his people is an important theme in Old Testament prophecy. Isaiah said, "Your Maker is your husband" (Isa. 54:5a). The prophet Hosea was commanded to marry Gomer the prostitute in order to show that God's people were "guilty of the vilest adultery in departing from the LORD" (Hos. 1:2). Predictably Gomer abandoned Hosea. Nevertheless God commanded the prophet to find her, buy her back, and love her all over again. Hosea was to "love her as the LORD loves the Israelites" (Hos. 3:1). The Bible uses this example to show how God intends to woo his beloved people back with tender words:

> "I will betroth you to me forever;
> I will betroth you in righteousness and justice,
> in love and compassion.
> I will betroth you in faithfulness,
> and you will acknowledge the LORD." (Hos. 2:19–20)

24

The prophet Jeremiah told much the same story. He depicted God on the witness stand in divorce court, fondly recalling his honeymoon: "I remember the devotion of your youth, how as a bride you loved me" (Jer. 2:2). But the honeymoon was a short one. Israel fell out of love, and God filed for divorce on the proper grounds of spiritual adultery. "You have lived as a prostitute with many lovers," he testified, "would you now return to me?" (Jer. 3:1). God's case against his people was watertight. The divorce was nearly finalized, but God never went through with it because his love is an everlasting love: " 'Return, faithless people,' declares the LORD, 'for I am your husband' " (Jer. 3:14). There is always a second honeymoon for the people of God.

The picture of marriage shows that the believer's relationship with Christ is an intimate, exclusive, and passionate covenant. The bond of our marital union with Christ is the unbreakable love of God, from which nothing can ever separate us (Rom. 8:38–39).

The vine, the body, and the marriage are not the only biblical pictures of union with Christ. Union with Christ is also compared with a covenant (Rom. 5:12–21), a household (Eph. 2:19–22), and a building (1 Peter 2:4–5). All of these images show what it is like to be in Christ. Union with Christ is a vital, life-giving, intimate relationship in which Jesus Christ is the source of life, authority, and everlasting faithfulness for the believer.

Union Incorporated

The biblical pictures of union and communion with Christ display the mystery of God's amazing grace, which grants us every spiritual blessing in Christ. There is something striking about all these pictures. One thing they share in common is that they are all corporate images. In other words, they do not show how one Christian is united to Christ; they show how *all* Christians are united to Christ.

Take the image of the vine and the branches. Jesus did not say, "I am the vine; you are the branch," as if he had only one disciple. Instead, he said, "I am the vine; you are the branches," thereby drawing all of his disciples together into one living plant.

Or consider the idea of the body. Jesus Christ is the head of the whole body; he is not united to only one appendage. The point Paul was trying to make for the Corinthians was that all the parts—nose, eyebrows, elbows, toenails, everything—are united together in one body: "Now the body is not made up of one part but of many" (1 Cor. 12:14). In the same way, through the unifying work of the Holy Spirit, all Christians are joined together in the body of Christ. In Calvin's words, "The elect are so united in Christ that as they are dependent on one Head, they also grow together in one body, being joined and knit together as are the limbs of a body."[10] The great Princeton theologian A. A. Hodge (1823–86) explained it like this: "Since all true believers are thus intimately united to Christ as the common Head of the whole body, and the Source of a common life, it follows that they must be intimately united together. If they have but one Head, and are all members of one body, they must have one common life, and be all members one of another."[11]

Even our marriage to Christ is not a private affair. Marriage is an exclusive relationship between one man and one woman. But whenever the Bible speaks about the marriage between Christ and the church, it always has the whole church in mind. The marriage described by Hosea and Jeremiah was a marriage between God and the nation of Israel. Likewise the mysterious marriage in Ephesians 5 is a marriage between Christ and the church, depicted as one immense bride.

The vine, the body, and the marriage show that all Christians everywhere are united to Christ together. Union with Christ is not a private enterprise. Although the Christian has a personal relationship with Jesus Christ, it is not a private relationship. We began this chapter by saying that there is no communion of the saints apart from their union with Christ. We have now arrived at an important conclusion: *There is no union with Christ without communion with the saints.* We cannot be united to Christ without also being united to every Christian. Union with Christ is not so much a union between Christ and the Christian as it is a union between Christ and the church. Thus it is better to speak of *our* union with Christ than *my* union with Christ. We are all in Christ together.

Union with Christ is the basis for the communion of the saints. If you were the only person united to Christ, then you could recite the Apostles' Creed like this: "I believe in the communion of the saint." Of course, then it would no longer be the Apostles' Creed; it would be Betty's Creed or Billy's Creed. And you would no longer have to go to Sunday morning worship to recite it. Betty and Billy could recite their personal creeds in their private homes. But we are not alone; we are not the only Christians united to Christ. The union and communion we enjoy with Jesus Christ are something we share together with all the saints, past, present, and future. For we believe in the communion of saints.

THREE

Baptized into Communion

*You are all sons of God through faith in Christ Jesus, for all of you
who were baptized into Christ have clothed yourselves with Christ.
(Gal. 3:26–27)*

*Saints by profession are bound to maintain an holy fellowship and
communion in the worship of God. (Confession of Faith, 26.2)*

The saints enter into union with Christ through baptism. When Paul
arrived at Ephesus he found disciples who had not yet received the
Holy Spirit. They had received only the baptism of John the Baptist,
a baptism of repentance. Because they had yet to receive the baptism
of faith, "they were baptized into the name of the Lord Jesus" (Acts
19:5). These disciples were not united to Jesus Christ until they were
united to him through baptism. This is true for all the saints: "All of
you . . . were baptized into Christ" (Gal. 3:27).

Baptism is what the Shorter Catechism terms an "ingrafting into
Christ" (Q. & A. 94). It symbolizes the death and burial of Jesus
Christ. Believers have "been buried with him [Christ] in baptism"
(Col. 2:12). The apostle Paul explained this symbolism to the Ro-
mans: "Don't you know that all of us who were baptized into Christ

Jesus were baptized into his death? We were therefore buried with him through baptism into death" (Rom. 6:3–4a). To be baptized is to be united to Jesus Christ in his death. However, since the purpose of this union is to participate in the life of Christ, baptism also unites us to Christ in his resurrection. As Paul goes on to explain, we were baptized into the death of Christ "in order that, just as Christ was raised from the dead through the glory of the Father, we too may live a new life. If we have been united with him like this in his death, we will certainly also be united with him in his resurrection" (Rom. 6:4b–5).

We have seen how the communion of the saints flows from our union with Christ. We can now apply this principle to baptism: Since believers are united to Christ through baptism, we are also united to one another through baptism. The saints enter into communion with one another through baptism.

Some Christians view baptism primarily as a private experience. In some churches baptism is viewed as a sign of one's personal faith in Jesus Christ. It is true that adult converts are to be baptized when they come to faith in Christ. But baptism is more than a sign of personal faith; it is a sign of union with Christ and communion with the saints. Baptism publicly signifies and confirms that we belong to Christ and to his community. John Calvin thus defined it as "the sign of the initiation by which we are received into the society of the church."[1]

The Scripture says that we share "one baptism" (Eph. 4:5). Perhaps it is for this reason that the Shorter Catechism insists on speaking of baptism in the plural (not "my ingrafting" but *our* ingrafting") when it teaches that baptism is a sacrament "wherein the washing with water in the name of the Father, and of the Son, and of the Holy Ghost, doth signify and seal our ingrafting into Christ, and the partaking of the benefits of the covenant of grace, and our engagement to be the Lord's" (Q. & A. 94). Much could be said about this pithy definition of baptism. Among other things, it reminds us that Christians are baptized in the triune name "of the Father and of the Son and of the Holy Spirit" (Matt. 28:19). But this chapter will concentrate on the definition's verbs: "washing," "signify," "seal," and "partake."

Washing with Water

One of the best ways to understand Protestant worship is to determine which passages of Scripture the church fathers and the Reformers had studied in regard to a particular question. The church fathers and the Reformers always insisted that they wanted to establish and reform their worship according to the Bible. It is best to take them at their word, so how did they understand the Scriptures in regard to baptism?

As early as the third and fourth centuries, whenever Christians explained the sacrament of baptism, they did so in terms of Noah's being saved from the flood and Israel's passage through the Red Sea. About the year 200 Tertullian (c. 165–215), a Roman lawyer who lived in Africa, wrote an essay on baptism. The essay is important because it is the first full treatment we have on the subject of baptism. Although it may seem strange to us, Tertullian explained baptism through a series of Old Testament types of baptism. A *type* is a person, practice, or event from the Old Testament that reveals the pattern of salvation in Jesus Christ.

By understanding baptism according to types, Tertullian was following the example of the New Testament. The earliest Christians understood baptism in terms of God's mighty acts of salvation by which he had saved his people Israel. Today we speak of these great events of the Old Testament as the types of redemption. The biblical types are really pictures. They are stories that tell us what something means. One way to explain salvation is to tell the story of how Moses led the people of Israel out of Egypt or how God saved Noah and his family from the wickedness of the world. These types are pictures of salvation that are carefully worked into the sacraments. Three types of redemption, each of which involved water, are especially relevant for baptism: the salvation of Noah and his family from the flood (Gen. 6–8); the passage of the people of Israel through the Red Sea (Exod. 13–14); and crossing the Jordan River into the Promised Land (Josh. 3–4).

First, the salvation of Noah is described in 1 Peter 3:20, where we are told that "only a few people, eight in all, were saved through water"; namely, Noah, his wife, his three sons, and their wives. The surprise comes in the following verse: "this water symbolizes baptism that now saves you also" (1 Peter 3:21). How does Christian baptism correspond to the salvation of Noah and his family from the great flood? Just as the sin of the world was washed away by the waters of the flood, so in our baptism we experience that same spiritual washing. It is not merely an outward washing away of dirt; it is rather a spiritual reality. Like Noah, we put our faith in God rather than in the ways of a sinful world for our salvation and thus participate in his saving grace.

When we are baptized, we are washed with the water of Noah's flood as a sign that we are now partakers in the salvation that God granted to Noah. When Noah and his family were sealed up in the ark and protected from the storm of God's judgment, they formed a communion of saints. Now we have been made members of that same community. The waters of baptism remind us of the waters of the flood. They are cleansing waters—waters that wash away sin.

The waters of the Red Sea are a second biblical type Christians have used to explain the sacrament of baptism. The earliest example of this is found in Paul's first letter to the Corinthians: "For I do not want you to be ignorant of the fact, brothers, that our forefathers were all under the cloud and that they all passed through the sea. They were all baptized into Moses in the cloud and in the sea" (1 Cor. 10:1–2). The phrase "were baptized into Moses" is surprising. It means that the passage through the Red Sea was a sort of baptism. By passing through the sea God's people were saved from their slavery in Egypt. In the same way, the saints are saved from their slavery to sin by passing through the waters of baptism. In other words, the crossing of the Red Sea was a type of baptism.

A third type or picture of baptism is the waters of the Jordan River. After forty years of wandering in the wilderness the children of Israel passed over the River Jordan and entered the Promised Land. Salvation consists not only of getting out of Egypt, the land of sin and slavery, but also of getting into the Promised Land, the land flowing with milk and honey.

The fact that Jesus was baptized in the Jordan River makes clear the relationship between the entrance into the Promised Land and Christian baptism. People often ask why Jesus, who was without sin, needed to be baptized (see Matt. 3:13–17). Some have suggested that this was his ordination as our high priest, and that as a true son of Israel, it was necessary for him to receive the ceremonial washing that set him apart for holy ministry. But part of the answer is that Jesus was the new Joshua. In fact, the two names (Jesus and Joshua) are the same name in two different languages: Greek and Hebrew. Joshua was a type of Jesus. Just as Joshua brought the children of Israel through the Jordan into the Promised Land, so Jesus led the way through baptism into the kingdom of God.

This was the shocking thing about the ministry of John the Baptist. John the Baptist called good Jews back into the wilderness. He took them into the wilderness to preach repentance to them. He was telling them that if they wanted to enter the kingdom of God, they had to leave the land, go out into the wilderness, be baptized in the Jordan River, and come back into the Promised Land. They had to start all over again spiritually. They had to become sons of Abraham by faith. In other words, they had to be born again. The sign of their new birth was washing with water, the water of the great flood, the

Red Sea, and the Jordan River all together. To be washed with the water of baptism is to become part of that community of God's people that follows Christ into the Promised Land.

Signify and Seal

What does it mean to say that baptism is a sacrament? The word *sacrament* was coined by Tertullian, who first called baptism a sacrament in his essay on baptism. Tertullian was a Roman citizen, so for him, a *sacramentum* was an oath made by a recruit to the army. Tertullian called baptism a sacrament because he understood that in baptism we make a pledge of loyalty to Christ as Lord. To be sure, baptism is a sign of our commitment to Christ, but that is not all. Baptism is primarily a sign of God's promise to us (which explains why the efficacy of baptism does not depend on the minister who performs it or on the church in which it is performed, but only on God's grace), and it is in this sense that we speak of baptism as a *sign*.

Two hundred years later another African Christian, Augustine (354–430), defined a sacrament as "an outward and physical sign of an inward and spiritual grace." For Augustine, a sacrament is a sign. It is not merely a symbol but also a sign in the biblical sense of the word: it points people to God's saving grace.

A good example of a biblical sign comes again from the story of Noah and the great flood:

> Then God said to Noah and to his sons with him: "I now establish my covenant with you and with your descendants after you and with every living creature that was with you—the birds, the livestock and all the wild animals, all those that came out of the ark with you—every living creature on earth. I establish my covenant with you: Never again will all life be

cut off by the waters of a flood; never again will there be a flood to destroy the earth."

And God said, "This is the sign of the covenant I am making between me and you and every living creature with you, a covenant for all generations to come." (Gen. 9:8–12)

The story of God purifying the world through a flood in the days of Noah is important for a true understanding of baptism. Baptism, like the rainbow, is a God-given sign of God's grace. It is a sign that seals a promise.

The biblical understanding of signs can also be illustrated from the story of God telling Abraham to circumcise his son. There circumcision is called "the sign of the covenant":

When Abram was ninety-nine years old, the LORD appeared to him and said, "I am God Almighty; walk before me and be blameless. I will confirm my covenant between me and you and will greatly increase your numbers."

Abram fell facedown, and God said to him, "As for me, this is my covenant with you: You will be the father of many nations. No longer will you be called Abram; your name will be Abraham, for I have made you a father of many nations. I will make you very fruitful; I will make nations of you, and kings will come from you. I will establish my covenant as an everlasting covenant between me and you and your descendants after you for the generations to come, to be your God and the God of your descendants after you. The whole land of Canaan, where you are now an alien, I will give as an everlasting possession to you and your descendants after you; and I will be their God."

Then God said to Abraham, "As for you, you must keep my covenant, you and your descendants after you for the generations to come. This is my covenant with you and your descendants after you, the covenant you are to keep: Every male among you shall be circumcised. You are to undergo circumcision, and it will be the sign of the covenant between me and you." (Gen. 17:1–11)

God gave Abraham a promise that he would be the God of Abraham's children as well as the God of Abraham. Circumcision was the sign of that covenant. The sign, like the covenant, was for children as well as their parents. Parents taught their children that circumcision was a visible reminder of the claims of God's grace.

It is important to notice that at the time God established the sign of the covenant he also gave Abraham and Sarah new names. This is why some Christians name their children at baptism. The Puritans loved to give their children biblical names. They also made a commitment to rear their children in the biblical way. Today many Reformed and Presbyterian churches take vows to assist parents in the Christian nurture of their covenant children. This is all part of what it means to practice the communion of the saints.

Finally, notice that circumcision is a sign of the covenant promise received by faith. The apostle Paul puts this very clearly: "And he [Abraham] received the sign of circumcision, a seal of the righteousness that he had by faith" (Rom. 4:11). This verse includes both of the words used in the Confession of Faith: "sign" and "seal." Baptism does not merely signify; it also seals. It seals the way that a signature seals a legal document. It is an official, visible confirmation of an inward, spiritual reality. Circumcision was not just a sign, therefore; it was a sign and a seal that made the covenant binding. It was an official, visible confirmation that someone belonged to the community of God's people. Ultimately, of course, the only way to belong to God's people was by faith, but circumcision was the outward sign and seal of that inward reality.

The New Testament clearly establishes a connection between circumcision and baptism. Circumcision is a type of baptism (which points to the validity of infant baptism): "In him [Christ] you were also circumcised, in the putting off of the sinful nature, not with a circumcision done by the hands of men but with the circumcision done by Christ, having been buried with him in baptism and raised with him through your faith in the power of God, who raised him from the dead" (Col. 2:11–12). The connection between circumcision and baptism could hardly be clearer. Circumcision prefigures baptism. The point of comparison is not so much the outward rite as it is the inward experience. Like circumcision, baptism is a sign and a seal of God's covenant. And like circumcision, baptism ultimately requires personal saving faith for its efficacy.

To summarize what we have been saying thus far, baptism marks a sinner's entrance into the communion of saints and seals that communion. As the English poet John Donne (1572–1631) wrote in one of his *Meditations*, when the church "baptizes a child, that action concerns me; for that child is thereby connected to that head which is my head too, and ingrafted into that body whereof I am a member."

Participating in the Covenant

The Westminster Confession of Faith teaches that baptism "signifies and seals our ingrafting into Christ and the partaking of the benefits of the covenant." The communion of saints means something more than simply having fellowship with others who are included in the covenant; it also means sharing together in the spiritual treasures promised in the covenant. We enjoy the benefits of the covenant because we participate in communion with Christ.

What are the benefits of the covenant? Many benefits could be mentioned. Forgiveness of sin, cleansing from guilt, deliverance from death, victory over Satan, and eternal life are all benefits of the covenant. The Shorter Catechism lists "assurance of God's love, peace of conscience, joy in the Holy Ghost, increase of grace, and perseverance therein" among the benefits that believers receive from their union with Christ (Q. & A. 36).

But the primary benefit of the covenant is God. The most basic promise of the covenant is this: "I will . . . be your God, and you will be my people" (see Lev. 26:12; Rev. 21:3). This is the covenant promise that God's people affirm whenever they gather for worship. Worship is the first responsibility of the covenant people, children as well as adults. This is clear from the first four commandments. We are to worship but one God; we are not to set up idols to help us worship; we are not to use God's name in vain; we are to remember and observe the Sabbath. Jesus summed this up by saying that the first great commandment is to love God (Matt. 22:37). That is what we do when we worship. We love God. We pour out our praise and adoration to him; we pour out our lamentations and confessions to him as well. Singing and weeping are both expressions of love to God.

To participate in the benefits of the covenant is to know God as Father. Hughes Oliphant Old has this to say about a father's heart:

> I have a nine-year-old son named Isaac. One of the things Isaac likes to do is have me put him to bed. We say that old prayer that has been passed down in Puritan families for centuries:
>
> > Now I lay me down to sleep.
> > I pray the Lord my soul to keep.
> > If I should die before I wake,
> > I pray the Lord my soul to take.
>
> Then very often Isaac will say, "Daddy, I want to have a man-to-man talk." Well, one time it is a mountain bike he wants,

blue, with curved-back handles. Then, another time it is a go-cart; then another time it is a Revolutionary War rifle. After a while I began to get sort of tired of all these "gimme, gimme" talks. I didn't say anything about it. I just listened and after a while I would say, "Well, son, it is time to go to sleep." Then one night, as he was going on about the mountain bike he wanted, it struck me: It is rather nice to have a little boy who looks to you for a mountain bike. That is what being a father is all about.

The covenant relationship between God and his people is a father/child relationship. To participate in the covenant is to go to our father for everything we need. It is because God is our God and we are his people that we go to him in time of need.

It is in terms of the covenant relationship that we are to understand that famous passage on baptism in Romans 6:

> Don't you know that all of us who were baptized into Christ Jesus were baptized into his death? We were therefore buried with him through baptism into death in order that, just as Christ was raised from the dead through the glory of the Father, we too may live a new life.
>
> If we have been united with him like this in his death, we will certainly also be united with him in his resurrection. For we know that our old self was crucified with him so that the body of sin might be done away with, that we should no longer be slaves to sin—because anyone who has died has been freed from sin.
>
> Now if we died with Christ, we believe that we will also live with him. (Rom. 6:3–8)

Baptism is not merely a dramatic portrayal of the burial and resurrection of Christ. It is not simply a ceremonial burial and rising up. For

Christians, baptism is a sign and a promise that all through life we will be washed from our sins by the work of the Holy Spirit in our hearts. It is a promise of continual spiritual cleansing so that more and more we will put to death the body of sin and come alive with new life.

Baptism is a sign given to us at the beginning of the Christian life promising that all our sins will be washed away. This can be illustrated from a final type, or biblical picture of baptism: Samuel anointing the boy David to be the king of Israel (1 Sam. 16). It is clear from the story that David was just a boy. How well did David understand the meaning of what the prophet was doing when he poured that oil on his head? Remember, Saul was still king in Israel. Would it not have been wiser to wait until David was a mature man before performing this sign? He would have understood it so much better!

That is not the way God did it. David was anointed when he was a mere lad. Years went by before he understood what it really means to be a king. And years went by before it even seemed possible for him to become king. As long as Saul reigned, his chances seemed remote. But the sign summed up David's destiny. In the providence of God, the sign meant that all God's promises for David would come true. He would partake of all the benefits and responsibilities of kingship.

As Christians we live under a sign, just as David did. The sign we live under is baptism. The promise we are given is the washing away of our sins and the receiving of the Holy Spirit. It was the promise made through the prophet Ezekiel: "I will sprinkle clean water on you, and you will be clean; I will cleanse you from all your impurities and from all your idols. I will give you a new heart and put a new spirit in you" (Ezek. 36:25–26). This is a promise for all God's saints, united to Christ, baptized in communion with one another.

FOUR

Members Only

You are no longer foreigners and aliens, but fellow citizens with God's people and members of God's household. (Eph. 2:19)

Saints, by profession, are bound to maintain an holy fellowship and communion. (Confession of Faith, 26.2)

Membership has its privileges. Even zoo membership has privileges, as trivial as they may seem. Members of the Philadelphia Zoo, for example, receive benefits that are not offered to the general public. They are invited to special events and lectures. They receive discounts on merchandise. They can visit the zoo during special evening hours. Best of all, once they become members they are welcome at the zoo as often as they go, without having to pay daily admission. Zoo membership is also optional. One does not have to be a zoo member to see the big cats or visit the reptile house. The whole zoo is open to the public. However, in the long run, it is more costly to visit the zoo without becoming a member.

Although the church is hardly a zoo (although one sometimes wonders), many of the same things can be said of church membership. There is a sense (only a very limited sense, as we shall see) in which being enrolled as an official member of a local church is optional. The basis for the communion of the saints is union with Christ by faith, not a listing in the church directory. However, failure to become a church member can be costly. This is because failure to become a church member or to take one's church membership seriously hinders the communion of the saints. And to the extent that a church's membership roll is an earthly copy, however imperfect, of the Lamb's Book of Life (Rev. 20:15), neglecting church membership calls one's salvation into question.

What the Church Is

We are beginning to understand the importance of the communion of saints. But who or what is the church — specifically, the visible church? Answering this question will help explain why church membership is essential to the communion of the saints.

The visible church is both smaller and larger than the communion of the saints. It is smaller because it does not include past or future saints but only those who presently are members of the church. However, it is larger because it includes unbelievers as well as believers. The communion of saints consists of true believers, all true believers, and only true believers. But the visible church is made up of all who say that they are Christians.

The Westminster Confession of Faith defines the church as follows: "The visible church, which is also catholic or universal under the gospel, consists of all those throughout the world that profess the true religion, together with their children; and is the kingdom of the Lord Jesus Christ, the house and family of God, out of which there is no ordinary possibility of salvation" (25.2). Several aspects of this definition have special relevance for church membership. The first is its identification of church members as those who "profess the true religion." This means that members have given a public testimony of faith in Jesus Christ. They have declared to the church that they are trusting in Christ alone for salvation, which is sometimes called making a "credible profession of faith." A credible profession includes a verbal testimony and a life that generally confirms the genuineness of that testimony (1 Cor. 1:2) and thus enables the church to make its corporate endorsement of an individual's salvation.

Pastors and elders of the church try to make sure that professions of faith are not merely credible but also true. Yet because of sin, especially secret sin, there are always some church members who are not truly saved. Some who profess Christ with their lips do not trust him in their hearts. Jesus warned his disciples that there will always be tares among the wheat and bad fish among the fresh catch (Matt. 13:24–30, 47–50). To use a contemporary metaphor, there is always junk mail mixed in with the personal correspondence. Or as Martin Luther liked to say, there will always be "mouse-droppings amongst the peppercorns."

The Confession of Faith defines the visible church as "the house and family of God." This is in keeping with Paul's description of Christians as "members of God's household" (Eph. 2:19), "those who belong to the family of believers" (Gal. 6:10). To call the church a house or a family reminds us that the children of believers are also members of the church. The visible church consists of those who profess faith in Christ "together with their children." This is because the church is a covenant community. In the Old Testament God established his covenant with the whole nation of Israel. The privileges and responsibilities of the covenant were for believers and for their children (Gen. 17:9–14). In the same way, the New Testament church is a covenant community. As Peter announced to the first Christians at Pentecost, "The promise is for you and your children" (Acts 2:39a). Scripture teaches that the children of the saints are holy to the Lord (1 Cor. 7:14).

43

When baptized children give a public testimony of their faith in Christ, they are not joining the church; they are already members. In this respect, church membership might be compared with citizenship in the United States of America. A child does not suddenly become an American citizen when he or she is old enough to vote. Rather, American children are born American. The same is true of the children of believers. Although they become communicant members (able to receive communion) when they profess their faith, they are members of the church of Jesus Christ from birth.

What the Church Does

The visible church is a household consisting of professing Christians and their children. But what does the church do? The Confession of Faith offers a short job description: "Unto this catholic visible church Christ hath given the ministry, oracles, and ordinances of God, for the gathering and perfecting of the saints in this life, to the end of the world; and doth by his own presence and Spirit, according to his promise, make them effectual thereunto" (25.3).

The main task of the church is to gather and perfect the saints. This is the mandate given to the church by Jesus Christ, sometimes known as the Great Commission. Jesus said, "Therefore go and make disciples of all nations, baptizing them in the name of the Father and of the Son and of the Holy Spirit, and teaching them to obey everything I have commanded you" (Matt. 28:19–20). Every true Christian church has the same mission statement: to proclaim the gospel message of salvation from sin through the death and resurrection of Jesus Christ (1 Cor. 15:1–4). The church is to take this message into all the world—making, baptizing and teaching followers for Jesus Christ. Evangelism, discipleship, and Bible teaching are thus essential activities of the local church.

The reason the church goes out into all the world is to gather the saints. This is one of the ways in which the communion of saints depends upon the church. It is the church's mission to draw the saints into communion with Christ and with one another. Practically speaking, it is impossible to be converted outside the ministry of the church. No one is ever saved alone but always through the church, into a vital connection with other believers. As Dietrich Bonhoeffer wrote, "No one can become a new man except by entering the Church, and becoming a member of the Body of Christ. It is impossible to become a new man as a solitary individual."[1]

Workers need the proper tools to complete a job, and church members are no exception. Christ has given the church three means to carry out its mission: "the ministry, oracles, and ordinances of God."

Ministry means primarily the pastoral ministry performed by the teaching and ruling elders of the church. Pastors and elders do not do all the work of the church by themselves, but their ministry is one of the primary means by which the church is enabled to carry out its mandate. God has called pastors and teachers "to prepare God's people for works of service, so that the body of Christ may be built up until we all reach unity in the faith and in the knowledge of the Son of God and become mature, attaining to the whole measure of the fullness of Christ" (Eph. 4:12–13).

The *oracles* of the church are the Scriptures of the Old and New Testaments. What ministers administer is the Word of God. The church proclaims and teaches the Bible. All of its evangelizing, preaching, teaching, worshiping, counseling, and serving are directed by the infallible Word of God. The saints are gathered by the proclamation of God's Word, and then they are perfected by putting into practice its teaching.

The *ordinances* of God are the sacraments of baptism and the Lord's Supper. Baptism is part of the gathering of the saints. As we have seen, believers enter the communion of the saints through baptism. The Lord's Supper is part of the perfecting of the saints. As the saints feed on the spiritual body and blood of Jesus Christ, they are nourished for Christian obedience.

The credibility of a church in the eyes of God depends on its proper use of these means. Some of its members may not be Christians. Remember the mouse droppings among the peppercorns! But a church is proven true or false depending upon its faithful use of these God-given means. G. I. Williamson writes, "A true Church visible is such, not because its membership is identical with the elect, but because it professes the true religion, maintains the teaching of the true doctrine and sacraments of the Scripture, and maintains the discipline required by the law of the Lord. Where there is fidelity in Word, sacraments, and discipline, there is the true visible Church."[2]

However, the means by which the church carries out its mandate—ministry, oracles, ordinances—do not operate by themselves. The effectiveness of these means depends upon the grace of God. It is Jesus Christ, "by his own presence and Spirit, according to his promise," who makes them effective. The ministers, Scriptures, and sacraments of the church operate through the power of Christ and the Holy Spirit.

How the Church Is Organized

The church is more than a loose association of people who share common interests. It is rather a family or household, and like all households, it has an organized structure. The head of this household is Jesus Christ. When Jesus gave the church its mandate, he began with these words: "All authority in heaven and on earth has been given to me" (Matt. 28:18). The church fulfills its mission under the authority of Jesus Christ, who is the sole and supreme Lord of the church.

One of the prerogatives of a leader is to delegate his authority, as Christ has done in the church: "The Lord Jesus, as King and Head of his church, hath therein appointed a government, in the hand of church officers" (Confession of Faith, 30.1). The biblical structure for church government is *presbyterian*. This term comes from the Greek word *presbuteros*, which means "elder." To say that the church is presbyterian is to say that the spiritual authority of the church resides in a body of elders. In his farewell address to the Ephesians, Paul referred to the church's leaders as "elders," "overseers" (or "bishops"), and "shepherds" (Acts 20:17, 28). The Bible uses these terms interchangeably to refer to the spiritual leaders of God's household. The biblical qualifications for elders are listed in 1 Timothy 3:1–7. They include integrity, fidelity, respectability, hospitality, peaceability, and charity. Men who meet these qualifications are ordained to govern (1 Tim. 5:17), to teach (2 Tim. 4:2), to shepherd (1 Peter 5:1–5), and to discern the Lord's will for the church (Acts 15).

The church's other office is deacon. Like the elders, the deacons are to be respectable, sincere, temperate, generous, and faithful (1 Tim. 3:8–13). The office of deacon is not an office of rule, however, but of service. Deacons are ministers of God's mercy inside and outside the church. They are servants; to employ the biblical term for deaconing (*diakonos*) in its most literal sense, they "wait on tables" (Acts 6:2). It is the high privilege of deacons to imitate the sacrificial ministry of Jesus Christ, who did "not come to be served, but to serve, and to give his life as a ransom for many" (Mark 10:45).

One of the responsibilities of church elders is to discipline church members according to the biblical pattern. Jesus said:

> If your brother sins against you, go and show him his fault, just between the two of you. If he listens to you, you have won your brother over. But if he will not listen, take one or two others along, so that "every matter may be established by the

testimony of two or three witnesses." If he refuses to listen to them, tell it to the church; and if he refuses to listen even to the church, treat him as you would a pagan or a tax collector. (Matt. 18:15–17)

Jesus outlines a three-step process that gradually moves from private admonition to public rebuke. To some this process may seem threatening. Christians usually think of church discipline only as excommunication for scandalous behavior. However, the biblical concept of discipline is broader and more positive. In fact, almost everything the elders do to give spiritual care to church members is a form of discipline. This is how the Presbyterian Church in America defines church discipline:

> Discipline is the exercise of authority given the Church by the Lord Jesus Christ to instruct and guide its members and to promote its purity and welfare. The term has two senses: the one referring to the whole government, inspection, training, guardianship and control which the Church maintains over its members, its officers and its courts; the other a restricted and technical sense, signifying judicial process.[3]

Preaching, teaching, and counseling are all forms of church discipline. Other forms of discipline include private rebuke, public admonition, and temporary suspension from the Lord's Table or other privileges of church membership.

Of course, a church member who persists in sin and stubbornly refuses to heed the counsel of elders ought to be excommunicated from the church. But even such stern discipline has a constructive purpose. It is intended to "produce a harvest of righteousness and peace" (Heb. 12:11) by drawing those who receive it back into the communion of the saints: "The power which Christ has given the

Church is for building up, and not for destruction. It is to be exercised as under a dispensation of mercy and not of wrath. . . . In this it acts the part of a tender mother, correcting her children for their good, that every one of them may be presented faultless in the day of the Lord Jesus."[4]

God's household works and plays by the rules given by Jesus Christ and administered by the officers of the church. The principle that underlies this structure is perhaps best expressed in Paul's command to the Corinthians: "Everything should be done in a fitting and orderly way" (1 Cor. 14:40). This verse is sometimes treated as a joke about the presbyterian love for church government. Nevertheless what this verse says is of crucial importance: everything the church does must be done "decently and in order," as the King James Version puts it. Church government is not a hindrance but a help to the communion of the saints. Christian communion flourishes in an orderly church.

Active Members

Now that we have determined what the church is, what it does, and how it is organized, we are able to learn what church members are to do. First, if the church consists of sinners who "profess the true religion," then its members are to believe the gospel of Christ and to live by it. We are to confess our sinfulness in God's sight, to believe that Jesus Christ died on the cross to atone for our sins, to fulfill the demands of the gospel by pursuing holiness in all our relationships, and to teach these gospel truths to others, especially our children.

Second, if the church is "the house and family of God," then we are called to join the household, to love our elder brother, Jesus Christ (Heb. 2:11–12), and to embrace all God's children as our brothers and sisters, showering them with all the love that family members deserve.

Third, if the church's mandate is to "gather and perfect the saints," then we are to pray for the lost, witness to our neighbors, and invite unsaved friends to church or to Bible study. We are to support the evangelistic ministries of the church with our time and money, and as new believers are brought into the church, to nurture them in the Christian faith. At the same time, we are to seek the sanctification of our souls through the means God has given: the Word and the sacraments. In other words, we must listen to our pastor's preaching and at the same time pray for his ministry and provide everything that his family needs (1 Tim. 5:17–18). We must read, study, meditate, obey, and pray through the Bible. We must also teach the Bible to others as we have opportunity. And we must observe the sacrament of baptism and participate regularly and reverently in the Lord's Supper.

Fourth, if the church has a divinely ordained structure, then we must conform to that structure. We are to elect church officers prayerfully and receive their counsel cheerfully. According to our gifts and God's call we may serve as officers. Regardless, we must remain spiritually accountable to our elders, submitting to their discipline in the Lord. We must gently restore others who have been caught in sin (Gal. 6:1). We must treat the church and its officers with love and respect. Churches do make mistakes. Church officers sometimes misinterpret the Bible, misdirect ministries, and mishandle discipline. Nevertheless the church and its officers deserve our love, humility, and respect: "Obey your leaders and submit to their authority. They keep watch over you as men who must give an account. Obey them so that their work will be a joy, not a burden, for that would be of no advantage to you" (Heb. 13:17). The church is the only earthly institution ever founded by Jesus Christ (Matt. 16:18). Its government has been established by God, through Christ, under the rule of his Word, for the redemption of the world. Therefore we must never undervalue the dignity and authority of the church.

When new members join Tenth Presbyterian Church in Philadelphia, they receive a booklet that offers a helpful summary of their responsibilities as active church members. New communicants are instructed:

1. To make diligent use of the *means of grace*, like the Christians of apostolic times, who "devoted themselves to the apostles' teaching and to the fellowship, to the breaking of bread and to prayer" (Acts 2:42).
2. To share faithfully in the *worship* of the church. "Let us not give up meeting together, as some are in the habit of doing, but let us encourage one another—and all the more as you see the Day approaching" (Heb. 10:25).
3. To share faithfully in the *service* of the church. "It was he [Christ] who gave some to be apostles, some to be prophets, some to be evangelists, and some to be pastors and teachers, to prepare God's people for works of service, so that the body of Christ may be built up" (Eph. 4:11–12).
4. To *give* of your substance as the Lord may prosper you. "On the first day of every week, each one of you should set aside a sum of money in keeping with his income, saving it up" (1 Cor. 16:2).
5. To give their whole heart to the service of Christ and his *kingdom* throughout the world, living lives "worthy of God, who calls you into his kingdom and glory" (1 Thess. 2:12).

Christians who make and keep these commitments honor God by strengthening the communion of saints.

Membership Has Its Privileges

One church bulletin included the following notice: "The Outreach Committee has enlisted 25 visitors to make calls on people who are not afflicted with any church." Belonging to a church may some-times seem like an affliction rather than an affiliation. When it does, it is tempting to ask whether there are any benefits to church mem-bership. In *Members One of Another*, Eric Lane urges us to resist this temptation:

> What difference will church membership make to me? is the question often in the mind (and sometimes on the lips). But it is the wrong question. The purpose of church membership is in relation to the church, not the individual. There are cer-tain aspects of the church which are meaningless without membership. At the same time church membership is cer-tainly of spiritual help to the believer in the living of the Christian life, . . . but this personal profit is a by-product and not the main end.[5]

If the church is established by God, ruled by Christ, and governed by the Word of his Spirit, then how can anyone refuse to join it? For Christians so to refuse is to fail to meet one of their fundamental obligations as followers of Christ.

Christians who resist the idea of formal membership sometimes question whether the Bible says that they officially have to join the church. However, it is clear from the New Testament that the first Christians believed in church membership and kept careful track of their members. Already at Pentecost, new converts were described as being "added to their number" (Acts 2:41, 47; 5:14). The appoint-ment of the first deacons was in response to the danger that some members who were on the rolls of the Jerusalem church were being overlooked (Acts 6:1–7). Timothy's church at Ephesus maintained a list of the widows under its care (1 Tim. 5:9), which is not surprising, given that the apostle Paul had addressed them as "members of God's household" (Eph. 2:19). When there was a case of grievous sin at

Corinth, Paul instructed the church to "put out of [their] fellowship the man who did this" (1 Cor. 5:2). He assumed that the elders could distinguish between those who were inside and those who were outside the church, a differentiation that requires fellowship on some sort of formal basis. Similarly the apostle John was able to discriminate between those who "belonged to us" and "did not really belong to us" (1 John 2:19). It only makes sense: If elders must "give an account" (Heb. 13:17), they must know for whom they are accountable. To put this another way, shepherds must know who their sheep are.

The church fathers also had strong views on church membership. Augustine argued that "without [the church] there is no forgiveness of sins."[6] Reformers like John Calvin believed the same thing:

> Let us learn even from the simple title "mother" how useful, indeed how necessary, it is that we should know her. For there is no other way to enter into life unless this mother conceive us in her womb, give us birth, nourish us at her breast, and lastly, unless she keep us under her care and guidance until, putting off mortal flesh, we become like the angels. . . . God's fatherly favor and the especial witness of spiritual life are limited to his flock, so that it is always disastrous to leave the church.[7]

The Puritans believed in church membership, too, although the Confession of Faith is more cautious than Calvin: "out of [the church] there is no ordinary possibility of salvation" (25.2). This wording suggests that in some extraordinary cases individuals may be saved without joining the church: inhabitants of remote islands, perhaps, or people who come to Christ for salvation on their deathbeds. Only in this very limited sense church membership may be considered optional. But outside of the church, there is no ordinary possibility of salvation.

A more contemporary example comes from R. B. Kuiper, who summarized much that we have been saying in this chapter:

> It is clear that in the days of the apostles it was universal practice to receive believers into the visible church.
>
> He who believes in Christ is united with Christ. Faith binds him to Christ. He is a member of Christ's body, the invisible church. But the visible church is but the outward manifestation of that body. Every member of the invisible church should as a matter of course be a member of the visible church. Extremely significant in this connection is Acts 2:47—"And the Lord added to the church daily such as should be saved." Not only does the Lord Christ require of those who are saved that they unite with the church; He Himself joins them to the church. And the reference is unmistakably to the *visible* church.
>
> Does it follow that he who is outside the visible church is necessarily outside Christ? Certainly not. It is possible that a true believer because of some unusual circumstance may fail to unite with the church. Conceivably one may, for instance, believe in Christ and die before receiving baptism. But such instances are exceptional. The Scriptural rule is that, while membership in the church is not a prerequisite of salvation, it is a necessary consequence of salvation. Outside the visible church "there is no ordinary possibility of salvation."[8]

Some Christians become actively involved in a local church without ever becoming members. It is good to become involved, but involvement without formal membership is like living together without getting married. To some people this seems like a good way to test the waters. They argue, "How can we know for sure if we are right for one another unless we live together for a little while? If things don't work out, then we can split up without a divorce." In addition to violating God's will for courtship and marriage, that approach is a well-known recipe for separation. Two people who only live together want the benefits of marriage without its safeguards. As a result, they lack the one thing that is crucial to a successful marriage (or to genuine sexual intimacy, for that matter): an unbreakable commitment to a mutual, inviolable covenant before God.

The same might be said of regular attenders who never join the church. They lack an unbreakable commitment to the church and its ministry. Nonmembers, however active they may be in the life of the church, are outside the covenant relationship with the body of Christ that God requires. They reserve the right to pick and choose their doctrine, lifestyle, and ministry. In effect they become their own elders, denying the authority of the church to carry out its mandate of gathering and perfecting the saints. To put this in theological terms, they separate union with Christ, the head of the church, from union with his body. As a result, they confuse themselves and others—outside as well as inside the church—about what it means to be a Christian. This is a costly mistake to make because membership has its privileges. Martyn Lloyd-Jones went so far as to describe church membership as "the biggest honour which can come a man's way in this world."[9] There is no union with Christ apart from the communion of the saints. Nor can the saints have true communion without belonging to one another by belonging to Christ in his church. The communion of the saints is for members only.

FIVE

United in Love

This is love: not that we loved God, but that he loved us and sent his Son as an atoning sacrifice for our sins. Dear friends, since God so loved us, we also ought to love one another. No one has ever seen God; but if we love one another, God lives in us and his love is made complete in us. (1 John 4:10–12)

All saints . . . being united to one another in love . . . have communion in each other. (Confession of Faith, 26.1)

It is an infamous fact that when Christian faith is in the minority, rather than banding together for the sake of strength, Christian leaders tend to compete. Protestant Christians in France are in the minority. Today they represent fewer than one million adherents in a country of some sixty million (a little more than 1 percent of the population). A much smaller number claims to be evangelical.

There were two world-class Protestant senior theologians in France during the twentieth century. Both were experts on John Calvin and the Genevan Reformation. One was a professor in a leading seminary and the other a pastor in the Reformed church. They were bitter enemies. Their dispute? Hard to say. They both adhered to the Confession of La Rochelle. They both loved the French wing of the Reformation and had written extensively on various aspects of it. One dispute that made it to the journals was over whether John Calvin had read any of the writings of Copernicus. One was persuaded he had and that his views of Genesis 1 reflected it. The other thought it likely that he had not. What was significant was not the issue. Scholars have been known to defend positions on even smaller matters with considerable passion. What was striking was the bitterness of the relentless criticisms they lodged against one another, in speech and in writing.

These two men grew old and went to their graves as bitter rivals. They were the main doctors of the tiny Reformed Church of France. Hundreds of believers looked to them for leadership and inspiration. What they will remember about them will include their contributions to theology. But they will especially remember their rivalry and their debates, sometimes amusing, more often harsh and caustic. The church remains small and ineffective to this day, and it cries out for solid teachers who can build up rather than destroy.

And in This Corner . . .

Christians have no monopoly on such feuding. It occurs in every profession and every institution. In government, political campaigns are infamous for avoiding ideas and attacking persons. In schools, disputes about ideas often lead to personal acrimony. In businesses, arguments over work and pay create a climate of hostility. Democrats and Republicans, faculty and administration, labor and management, husbands and wives, parents and children . . . why can't we just get along?

Who is the rival in your life? Who is your nemesis? Is it a colleague? A boss? A relative? We all have enmities like these. They may be so-called friendly rivalries. They may come from simply misreading someone's intentions. Other enmities are deep, leading to a lifelong slavery to hatred. Occasionally they lead to violence. More often they are just there: gnawing, unresolved altercations. They may go on until death, when it is too late for public reconciliation. What is missing is love, the primary mark of life in Christ.

The Bible is realistic about the tragedy of personal conflict. Though dreadful, the problem of strife is not surprising. Though sad, it is not strange. Human enmity is discussed over and over in the pages of Scripture: Jacob and Esau (Gen. 25:19–34), Saul and David (1 Sam. 18–26), Euodia and Syntyche (Phil. 4:2–3). Rivalry is as old as Cain and Abel (Gen. 4), and behind that, the enmity between the children of God and the serpent (Gen. 3). Strife comes from sin. When two or more people do not get along, it is a sign that we are still living in a fallen world, under the regime of sin.

The real surprise is that people ever get along well. Harmony replacing rivalry is a sign of nothing less than heaven on earth. It is a manifestation of divine love, which is why it is found most frequently and most genuinely in the communion of saints, who are united in God's love. As Augustine wrote in his commentary on the Book of Genesis, "There are, then, two loves, of which one is holy, the other unclean; one turned towards the neighbor, the other centered on self; one looking to the common good, keeping in view the society of saints in heaven, the other bringing the common good under its own power."[1] Because it is selfless and holy, the love of God enables the saints to love one another.

The Basis of Love

Reconciliation seems so hard that many are tempted to leave well enough alone and hope for the best. But the good news of the gospel is that God, in providing the great remedy for sin, has also provided a glorious solution to the problem of human conflict. It is reconciliation and harmony in Jesus Christ. When God "was reconciling the world to himself in Christ" (2 Cor. 5:19), he was also reconciling us to one another.

The Westminster Confession of Faith correctly conjoins communion with one another to communion with Christ. Union with Christ unites the saints in love. Luther claimed that when Christians say, "I believe in the communion of saints," they are confessing "that there is on earth a little holy flock or community of pure saints under one head, Christ. It is called together by the Holy Spirit in one faith, mind, and understanding. It possesses a variety of gifts, yet is united in love."[2]

We are not "united in love," as Luther put it, simply because once we are saved it then makes sense to engage in communal duties. The Christian church is not merely a convenient way for individuals to practice their social piety. Rather, we are united in love because we are united to Christ by the Holy Spirit through faith. The Puritan Richard Sibbes (1577–1635) put it like this: "As we are knit to Christ by faith, so we must be knit to the communion of saints by love."[3] There is no other kind of new life but common life, because fellowship with Christ in his graces, sufferings, death, resurrection, and glory is communal. We enjoy his graces by sharing our gifts. We participate in his sufferings by carrying one another's burdens.

The writers of the twenty-sixth chapter of the Confession of Faith were perhaps meditating on Ephesians 4 as they wrote. This section is an extended exhortation to live in communion, to be "united in love." As he inevitably does, Paul shows that this communion and this love are already a reality. The communion of saints is not something we must create but something we receive as a gift from God's Spirit. God has given us to one another in love. Now the communion that we have been given needs to be developed and maintained. We should become what we already are in Christ, living a life worthy of the calling that we have received (Eph. 4:1). We already are united in love; now we must live out this unity until it becomes fully manifest. To that end, we must pray for ourselves the way that Paul prayed for the Thessalonians: "May the Lord make your love increase and overflow for each other and for everyone else" (1 Thess. 3:12).

The Life of Love

The Greek word *koinonia* ("communion") is rich with meaning. In biblical times it was used to describe human sharing in business, law, citizenship, marriage, and friendship. One of its synonyms is "conversation." It has an active connotation. The true meaning of communion is not passive basking but active fellowship. It is hard for modern people to live in community. One irony of modernity is that it forces us together but without true conversation. We interact with an unprecedented number of people but commune with few of them. Rapid transportation and instant communication give only the illusion of community. Whether on the telephone or in cyberspace, we talk to people near and far but rarely engage them in meaningful personal intercourse. Sociologists tell us that Americans are going indoors or cocooning in the privacy of their homes. We can do almost everything at our desks, never having to meet other people and rub elbows with them. We are like people who find themselves thrown together on an elevator: we may be traveling to the same place but our eyes never meet. Nor do our hearts.

Facing someone with open eyes and an open heart is one of the most difficult of all human practices. Years ago there was a polemic between two professors at a prominent seminary. It became rather heated as they wrote articles attacking each other's positions. At one point when a particular argument had been advanced, a student innocently asked one professor what his colleague had to say in response. His answer was as surprising as it was tragic. He said that he

61

did not know, because they had never talked about their polemic in all their years of teaching together.

This is how bitter disputes usually come about, especially in the church. They begin with a statement, a rumor, or an impression. Then each side locks in. As some politicians do, we put our opponent on our list of enemies. We do everything we can to avoid the person. The disagreement becomes a dispute. We still avoid contact; now it becomes harder to go back. The dispute becomes a controversy. We hope we never see the other person again. And so it goes, until death intervenes. Then guilt and regret set in, but nothing can be done.

In Ephesians 4 the apostle Paul gives us powerful instructions for avoiding or correcting conflict in the church:

> Be completely humble and gentle; be patient, bearing with one another in love. Make every effort to keep the unity of the Spirit in the bond of peace. (Eph. 4:2–3)

> Speaking the truth in love, we will in all things grow up into him who is the Head, that is, Christ. From him the whole body, joined and held together by every supporting ligament, grows and builds itself up in love, as each part does its work. (Eph. 4:15–16)

> "In your anger do not sin": Do not let the sun go down while you are still angry, and do not give the devil a foothold. (Eph. 4:26–27)

> Do not let any unwholesome talk come out of your mouths, but only what is helpful for building others up according to their needs, that it may benefit those who listen. (Eph. 4:29)

> Get rid of all bitterness, rage and anger, brawling and slander, along with every form of malice. Be kind and compassionate

to one another, forgiving each other, just as in Christ God forgave you. (Eph. 4:31–32)

All the vices that create conflict are condemned: anger, slander, and malice. All the virtues that prevent conflict are commanded: humility, love, and kindness. All the graces that heal conflict are commended: patience, compassion, and forgiveness. These instructions are summed up in the following words from Scripture: "live a life of love, just as Christ loved us and gave himself up for us" (Eph. 5:2).

We are involved with one another whether we like it or not. This is what Paul means by "bearing with one another" (Eph. 4:2). To paraphrase, we must put up with one another. We must do this because we are in Christ, and love is what it means to be a believer. Is this hopeless idealism? Burdensome law? One young man was brought up by a traditionally minded mother. In keeping with her tradition she gave her children a motto. His was, "Be Ye Kind One to Another." He grew to hate the motto, always suspecting its real purpose was to keep him from fights with his brother. It was only well into adulthood, after becoming a believer in Christ, that he realized the real problem with his motto. It was taken out of its biblical context. The motto, which comes from Ephesians 4:32, was moralistic because it was detached from the rest of the Book of Ephesians. It was law without grace. It looked for the fruit of spiritual communion apart from the root of union with Christ.

It takes grace to go to someone who disagrees with you and try to resolve the conflict. But we have that grace in Christ, who said, "First go and be reconciled to your brother; then come and offer your gift" (Matt. 5:24). It takes grace to reach out to your most dreaded antagonist with love. But we have that grace. It takes supernatural power to go out and help someone you would rather not deal with. It takes a deep understanding of what is at stake to go and seek the forgiveness of someone whom you do not care to acknowledge. It may take even more grace to offer forgiveness. But we can forgive, because we know the forgiveness of Christ. Christ who died on the cross is alive today, with resurrection power, to equip us for the ministry of reconciliation.

The Urgency of Love

One of the most famous rivalries of the nineteenth-century literary world was between William Makepeace Thackeray and Charles Dickens.[4] Both were superb writers, praised and acknowledged in their day as well as ours. Their styles were different, but both men were successful enough that their audiences assured them fame.

Their rivalry began when a young writer named Edmund Yates wrote a most unflattering column about Thackeray in the gossip sheet *Town Talk*, focusing on his person and character. The article was typical of the material in that kind of tabloid and ordinarily would have been ignored. But Thackeray—whose middle name, Makepeace, did not guide him on these occasions—shot back a vitriolic response.

It happened that at the same time Dickens was having domestic difficulties. He had moved his wife out of the house and provided her with a stipend, an action for which he was criticized by a number of Londoners. Dickens's response was to keep a mental list of enemies who did not deserve his friendship. Thackeray was among them because he had made some tactless remarks about his rival's marital situation. So when the occasion came, Dickens chose to help Yates with his polemics. Yates now had one of the world's greatest novelists ghost writing for him. To make matters worse, all three men were members of the Garrick Club, a respectable men's establishment. Rivalry was considered a breach of gentlemanly demeanor and therefore unworthy of club members. Thackeray thus brought a complaint to the board of governors of the Garrick asking them to discipline Yates. Yates agreed to apologize to the board yet refused to apologize to

Thackeray. In the end he was ejected from the club, and Dickens, the real subject of the feud, was furious.

The two great writers remained enemies until Thackeray's death. Almost. There is a warm, nearly pathetic end to the story. The daughters of the two men were good friends. Thackeray enjoyed Dickens's daughter Kate so much that he would often call on her. Because of his admiration for Dickens as a writer, he would ask Kate questions about her father's literary technique. Eventually Thackeray persuaded her to admit Dickens was more in the wrong than he, but she excused her father on account of his shyness and awkwardness in frank, personal discussions. So the enmity went on, but less intensely. Finally, just a few days before his death, Thackeray chanced upon his rival and held out his hand. According to Kate, Dickens did not say anything but grasped Thackeray's hand with tears in his eyes. At the graveside, Dickens was visibly shaken by what was left undone in their relationship.

The apostle Paul urges us to seek reconciliation as soon as we can, while there is still time, as a way of exhibiting our union with Christ. Christian unity is not merely a feeling; nor is it a mystical bond without earthly implications. It involves many practical applications in the church. It takes the patience and mercy of God for a church to decide what kind of music to use in worship, or which evangelistic approach is most appropriate, or how to spend a sum of money that comes as a bequest. It takes the power of grace to talk with brothers and sisters from Christian traditions different from our own. But when it comes to reconciliation, the Bible never lets us off the hook. Love is not an option. Indeed, it is the most basic command of Christ: "Love one another" (John 13:34; cf. 1 John 3:11).

The Confession of Faith states that the loving communion of the saints is to be extended to "all those who in every place call upon the name of the Lord" (26.2). This includes loving other Christian denominations, or practicing ecumenism, as it is called. To be sure, ecumenical dialogues will sometimes be polemical. The Bible never allows us to sacrifice biblical truth for Christian unity, as some do. It teaches us to "speak the truth in love" (Eph. 4:15), which preserves the purity and the unity of the church. But to speak the truth in love, we must first speak. And we must speak with the express purpose of getting together. It is easy to think of a thousand reasons for avoiding the true dialogue of love. It is more comfortable to follow the trend, going indoors in the name of communication. But we have the love of Christ, who showed us how to love the unlovely. Likewise we must find ways to commune with all the saints.

The Grace of Love

Isn't reconciliation just for some Christians? Isn't it a special calling for more sensitive believers? What do we lose if we put reconciliation on the back burner? The answer is that refusal to commune with one another is deeply sinful. The apostle Paul identifies the particular sin in failing to love the saints. Surprisingly he does not focus on hatred or anger, although he does mention those sins. Instead, he names another, related sin: immaturity. If we stay where we are and never work together, then we are infants (Eph. 4:14). We are unstable, wide open to any doctrine or power scheme that blows in the wind. Children are cute and adorable . . . as long as they are children. But how sad to observe children who never grow up. How unnatural are older persons who, like Peter Pan, in the name of freedom never leave childhood. Refusing to find the green fields of maturity is the opposite of freedom. It is slavery to self.

Loveless immaturity is particularly offensive among the saints, because God intends the church to be a showpiece of his love. "By this all men will know that you are my disciples," said Jesus, "if you love one another" (John 13:35). In his wonderful book on Christian love, *The Mark of the Christian*, Francis Schaeffer (1912–84) commented that without true Christians loving one another, Christ says the world cannot be expected to listen, even when we give proper answers. Let us be careful, indeed, to spend a lifetime studying to give honest answers. . . . But after we have done our best to communicate to a lost world, still we must never forget that the final apologetic which Jesus gives is the observable love of true Christians for true Christians. . . . If the world does not see this, it will not believe that Christ was sent by the Father.[5]

Where can we get this evangelistically essential love? Only from God, and only by the grace that he has shown in Jesus Christ. One of the great heresies today is the heresy of love. It says that love is God and that with a little bit of love everything else will fall into place. Ironically, with all the talk of love there is little of the thing itself. We say, "It takes a village," but we live as individuals. We talk about family values, but we know little about the value of a family. We live in a graceless age, in which people resolve their conflicts either by avoidance or by anger. But anger, though occasionally righteous, is never a cure. Only grace is. We live in a graceless age, in which we forget that every good thing we have is a gift from God. Anything good in this life is by the grace of God in Jesus Christ, whose death and resurrection mean the way is open to communion and conversation.

Love is not God, but God is love. The fullness for which we strive is nothing less than Jesus Christ, the head from which and unto which we must grow in love. We have that grace now, as much as we need of it, and more. We are one in Christ Jesus. But we must reach for full unity in the faith and knowledge of Christ. The great joy of this faith and knowledge is having it together with all the saints, past, present, and future. We are all united in love to that same Lord Jesus Christ who at Calvary gave up his communion and conversation with the Father in order to give them to us.

SIX

Assembly Required

They devoted themselves to the apostles' teaching and to the fellow-
ship, to the breaking of bread and to prayer. (Acts 2:42)

Saints by profession are bound to maintain an holy fellowship and
communion in the worship of God. (Confession of Faith, 26.2)

The communion of saints is closely related to the celebration of worship. The Westminster Confession of Faith teaches that one of the primary ways for the saints "to maintain an holy fellowship and
communion" is in "the worship of God" (26.2). The communion of
the saints is of the essence of Christian worship.

When the worship historian Hughes Oliphant Old visited Korea
to lecture on the history of Christian worship, he explored the city of
Seoul. He attended Christian churches scattered across the city and
found that Korean services were much like ones that he had attended
in America. But he also wanted to see something different. He writes:

> Being a real tourist I wanted to see a Buddhist temple. In the
> center of town there was only one Buddhist temple. I
> searched it out, and I was surprised how small it was. There

were many people there doing private devotions but no sacred assembly where everyone came together for church. Buddhism, unlike Christianity, has no coming together of the church for common worship.

The experience served to remind Old that Christian worship at its core is a communion, a coming together of a sacred assembly for the purpose of serving God's glory.

Worship as Communion

By emphasizing fellowship, the Westminster Divines picked up on a basic biblical teaching about Christian worship. This is how the earliest church worshiped: "They devoted themselves to the apostles' teaching and to the fellowship, to the breaking of bread and to prayer" (Acts 2:42). This text teaches that the worship of the earliest Christians included four things. First, there was the teaching and preaching of the apostles. Second, there was what is simply called "the fellowship." Third, there was the breaking of bread, or the celebration of the Lord's Supper. Fourth, there were the prayers, which seems to refer to public prayers offered at the temple morning and evening.

The second of these four elements is termed "the fellowship." As we learned in chapter 5, the Greek word used for fellowship is *koinonia*. *Koinonia* is the biblical term that underlies the doctrine of the communion of saints. Sometimes the word is translated as "fellowship," sometimes as "communion," and sometimes even as "sharing." However the Greek word is translated, it expresses an important biblical concept: God's glory is served by the fellowship of Christians—the communion of the saints. When Christians come together in a sacred assembly, when they are united together in their love for one another, when they are at one in their faith, and when they share their spiritual and material goods with one another, then God is worshiped in Spirit and in truth. The New Testament word *koinonia* encompasses all of this.

To understand the historical roots of Protestant worship the place to go is Strasbourg, which is what John Calvin did when he set about the reform of worship in Geneva. Calvin took the Reformed Church of Strasbourg as his model. Worship in Strasbourg had been reformed under the leadership of Martin Bucer (1491–1551). At the end of 1524 Bucer wrote an explanation of his liturgical reforms in *Grund und Ursach* ("Basic Reasons"). This reform had been in progress for more than a year before Martin Luther made any changes in the worship of the Church of Wittenberg. Bucer found in Acts 2:42 the biblical basis for the reform of worship. A truly reformed worship should include the preaching and teaching of God's Word, prayer, the sacraments, and *koinonia*, which is the fellowship of the congregation. At one point Bucer even tried to get the whole population of Strasbourg into the cathedral for a single communion service each Lord's Day, but the people resisted. It has never been easy to practice the communion of the saints!

Communion on the Mountain

The worship of Israel at the foot of Mount Sinai makes it clear that the communion of the saints is of the essence of Christian worship. This story, recorded in Exodus 24, is the earliest service of public worship in the Bible. It took place when Israel came together as a sacred assembly to hear the reading of the law that God had revealed to Moses:

When Moses went and told the people all the LORD's words and laws, they responded with one voice, "Everything the

LORD has said we will do." Moses then wrote down everything the LORD had said.

He got up early the next morning and built an altar at the foot of the mountain and set up twelve stone pillars representing the twelve tribes of Israel. Then he sent young Israelite men, and they offered burnt offerings and sacrificed young bulls as fellowship offerings to the LORD. Moses took half of the blood and put it in bowls, and the other half he sprinkled on the altar. Then he took the Book of the Covenant and read it to the people. They responded, "We will do everything the LORD has said; we will obey."

Moses then took the blood, sprinkled it on the people and said, "This is the blood of the covenant that the LORD has made with you in accordance with all these words."

Moses and Aaron, Nadab and Abihu, and the seventy elders of Israel went up and saw the God of Israel. Under his feet was something like a pavement made of sapphire, clear as the sky itself. But God did not raise his hand against these leaders of the Israelites; they saw God, and they ate and drank. (Exod. 24:3–11)

Several things should be noticed from this report. First, we learn that Moses wrote down in a book the words that God had spoken to him. This book no doubt included the Ten Commandments as well as their interpretation, as found in Exodus 21–23. After the reading of the law the people vowed to keep this Book of the Covenant (Exod. 24:7).

Second, we notice the rite of sprinkling. Sacrifices were made, and the blood from the sacrifices was sprinkled first on the altar and then on the people. What is the significance of this rite? It indicates the strong unity between those who participated in it. The community is tied together by blood. But notice that the blood is not sprinkled on the members of the assembly only. Half the blood was sprinkled on the altar; that is, symbolically it was sprinkled on God. God and his people are united together in a blood relationship.

The blood relationship is also a covenant relationship. Moses tells the people that the blood he sprinkles is "the blood of the covenant" (Exod. 24:8). A covenant relationship is a spiritual bond, a unity that comes through sharing a common faith. It is a supernatural love commitment stronger than any natural, blood relationship. The sacred assembly that hears the word of God and vows to obey it worships, because the covenant is established and nourished by worship. Furthermore, the covenant relationship is established "in accordance with all these words" (Exod. 24:8). Thus the reading and preaching of Scripture are essential to worship and the covenant relationship.

The third thing we notice from the worship at Mount Sinai is the covenant meal on the top of the mountain. This text is remarkable: "They saw God, and they ate and drank" (Exod. 24:11). Here too the significance of the rite is the unity that is established between those who share a meal. To share a meal with someone is to enter into the same family. We find covenant meals all through the Bible. Their purpose is to bring those who share them into communion with one another. Melchizedek, king of Salem, went out to meet Abraham as he returned from his victory in the battle of the kings. Melchizedek prepared a meal for Abraham to establish an alliance of peace with him (Gen. 14:17–24). Abraham did the same thing when the three heavenly visitors came to tell him of the future God had in store for him (Gen. 18:1–15). So also Jesus, before he entered into his passion, ate the Passover with his disciples in the upper room (Matt. 26:20–29). He shared this meal with them to show that everything he was about to do would be for them. Then, having risen victorious on the third day, he again shared a meal with two of his disciples on the

Emmaus road. He did this to unite them to himself in his death and his resurrection (Luke 24:13–43).

The meal on the mountain in Exodus 24 was the same kind of meal. It gives a picture of what worship is supposed to be. Worship is communion. By assembling together as the covenant community, the saints enter into a sacred communion with each other and with God. The Book of the Covenant is read, vows are made to live by the teachings of this book, the people are sprinkled with the blood of the covenant, and a meal is shared to seal the covenant relationship.

Worship is best understood in covenant terms. In other words, worship is best understood from the standpoint of the communion of the saints. It is through worship that the saints enter and are built up into communion with one another. This is why the fourth commandment is essential to the Christian faith: "Remember the Sabbath day by keeping it holy" (Exod. 20:8). Every week the faithful are taught to come together in a sacred assembly to remember God's mighty acts of creation and redemption (Exod. 20:11; Deut. 5:15). This is how the church experiences the communion of the saints, which is why we must not "give up meeting together" (Heb. 10:25). Assembly is required. As John Wesley once observed, "There is nothing more unchristian than a solitary Christianity."[1]

Communion in the City

A second passage of Scripture that explains the communion of the saints is the story of the sacred assembly held in Jerusalem during the days of Nehemiah. When the exiles returned from Babylon, the people of God met in the plaza at the water gate to restore the sacred community that had been scattered under Nebuchadnezzar. They understood that assembly was required.

When the seventh month came and the Israelites had settled in their towns, all the people assembled as one man in the square before the Water Gate. They told Ezra the scribe to bring out the Book of the Law of Moses, which the LORD had commanded for Israel.

So on the first day of the seventh month Ezra the priest brought the Law before the assembly, which was made up of men and women and all who were able to understand. He read it aloud from daybreak till noon as he faced the square before the Water Gate in the presence of the men, women and others who could understand. And all the people listened attentively to the Book of the Law. (Neh. 8:1–3)

This worship assembly was important enough for Nehemiah to describe in careful detail:

Ezra the scribe stood on a high wooden platform built for the occasion. Beside him on his right stood Mattithiah, Shema, Anaiah, Uriah, Hilkiah and Maaseiah; and on his left were Pedaiah, Mishael, Malkijah, Hashum, Hashbaddanah, Zechariah and Meshullam.

Ezra opened the book. All the people could see him because he was standing above them; and as he opened it, the people all stood up. Ezra praised the LORD, the great God; and all the people lifted their hands and responded, "Amen! Amen!" Then they bowed down and worshiped the LORD with their faces to the ground.

The Levites—Jeshua, Bani, Sherebiah, Jamin, Akkub, Shabbethai, Hodiah, Maaseiah, Kelita, Azariah, Jozabad, Hanan and Pelaiah—instructed the people in the Law while the people were standing there. They read from the Book of the Law of God, making it clear and giving the meaning so

that the people could understand what was being read.
(Neh. 8:4–8)

The people's response was equally noteworthy:

> Then Nehemiah the governor, Ezra the priest and scribe, and
> the Levites who were instructing the people said to them all,
> "This day is sacred to the LORD your God. Do not mourn or
> weep." For all the people had been weeping as they listened
> to the words of the Law.
>
> Nehemiah said, "Go and enjoy choice food and sweet
> drinks, and send some to those who have nothing prepared.
> This day is sacred to our Lord. Do not grieve, for the joy of the
> LORD is your strength." The Levites calmed all the people, say-
> ing, "Be still, for this is a sacred day. Do not grieve." Then all
> the people went away to eat and drink, to send portions of food
> and to celebrate with great joy, because they now understood
> the words that had been made known to them. (Neh. 8:9–12)

The sacred assembly included men, women, and children (Neh. 8:3).
The fact that everyone was included is important. On the one hand were
the children and on the other were the elders; in fact, the elders are mentioned by name. It was important who was on the platform because this
made clear that it was an official assembly. Anyone who has watched a political convention will recognize the significance of being on the platform.

Second, the main event is the reading through of the whole of
Scripture. It took all morning long every day for a week. Not only
were the Scriptures read, but they were also explained. We have here
both the reading of the lesson and the preaching of the sermon (Neh.
8:8). This passage shows that the community was reconstituted
through hearing the reading and the preaching of God's Word.

Third, certain rites associated with the reading of the law mark this occasion as a service of worship. Anyone who has attended a synagogue service recognizes them immediately. The Scripture says that Ezra opened the book in the sight of the people (Neh. 8:5). This may refer to the holding up of the scroll so everyone could see it. With this everyone stood. Ezra offered prayer and the people said "Amen! Amen!" (Neh. 8:6). These are rites that had been practiced for generations in the sacred assemblies of Israel. They were not innovations. They were not traditions invented on the spot by Ezra. The reading of Scripture was at the center of worship. This was not simply a lecture or a seminar; it was the official worship of the covenant community.

Finally, we notice that the reading and preaching were concluded by a feast. Presumably this feast was held in individual homes. Yet Nehemiah instructed the people to send "portions" to friends and neighbors who were in need. Apparently the exchanging of dishes was a feature of the feast. Once again a common meal is used as a means of sealing the unity of the covenant community. The concern shown here for the poor introduces a theme to which we shall return in chapter 9, "Relief in Outward Things."

Rabbinic tradition counts the service at the Water Gate as the first synagogue service. Be that as it may, the occasion shows that Israel understood its worship as a covenantal act. Worship is an experiencing of the covenantal community, a realization of the communion of the saints. It is exactly what the Confession of Faith has in mind when it says that the saints "are bound to maintain an holy fellowship and communion in the worship of God" (26.2).

Communion in the Church

Like worship on the mountain and in the city, worship in the church is a communion of saints. The church follows the pattern for covenant worship God first established through Moses and Ezra.

We have already noticed the importance of the fellowship (*koinonia*) of worship in the early church. The first Christians "devoted themselves to the apostles' teaching and to the fellowship, to the breaking of bread and to prayer" (Acts 2:42). The Scripture goes on to describe several ways that they put the communion of saints into practice: "All the believers were together and had everything in common. . . . Every day they continued to meet together in the temple courts. They broke bread in their homes and ate together with glad and sincere hearts" (Acts 2:44, 46). The first Christians shared a common life. They established a learning, caring, worshiping, growing community in which they did everything together: willingly they donated their possessions, joyfully they shared their meals, and daily they assembled at the temple for worship. As Gene Getz has explained, the Book of Acts teaches far more "about corporate prayer, corporate learning of biblical truth, corporate evangelism, and corporate Christian maturity and growth than about the personal aspects of these Christian disciplines."[2] The first Christians understood that within the communion of the saints, covenant assembly is required.

The necessity of worshiping as a community is reinforced elsewhere in the New Testament. Jesus made regular practice of going to the synagogue for worship (see Luke 4:16). The apostle Paul refers to the worship services in Corinth as "coming together as a church" (1 Cor. 11:18). Part of his point is that the assembly of the Christian community is of the essence of Christian worship. Within the communion of the saints, assembly is required. The writer to the Hebrews makes the same point: "Let us consider how we may spur one another on toward love and good deeds. Let us not give up meeting together, as some are in the habit of doing" (Heb. 10:24–25).

Meeting together is necessary for two reasons. One is for the sake of others. Our presence at the assembly is required to spur them on to love and good deeds. But this is also good for ourselves. Our presence at the assembly renews our commitment to the covenant community. The Puritan Robert Harris (1581–1658) exhorted his parishioners, "Especially apply your selves to the communion of the Saints: A dead coal, put [next] to live coals, will take fire from them, which it would never do lying in the dead heap: so here . . . sort yourselves with such as are godly, and frequent the ordinances [preaching, prayer, and the sacraments] . . . that you may have part in the new covenant."[3]

In the church, as on the mountain and in the city, worship should be viewed from a covenant standpoint. This is true for congregational singing, in which God's people give praise to their God with one voice. In one of the earliest extrabiblical descriptions of Christian worship, written around A.D. 112, Pliny explained to the Roman emperor Trajan that Christians "were in the habit of meeting on a certain fixed day before it was light, when they sang an anthem to Christ as God."[4] Christians have been singing ever since, enjoying sweet communion in musical praise. As the nineteenth-century historian and theologian Philip Schaff once observed, "The church-hymn is one of the most powerful means for promoting the *unity* of the faith and the *communion* of the saints."

Prayer should also be viewed from a covenantal vantage point. It is characteristic of Christian prayer that the saints pray together. When Jesus taught his disciples to pray he did not say, "My Father, who art in heaven." Instead, he taught us to pray in the first person plural: "Our Father in heaven" (Matt. 6:9). The Lord's Prayer is a prayer for the whole community of saints. The first Christian prayer meeting recorded in the Acts of the Apostles featured corporate prayer. When the believers heard that Peter and John had been released from prison, "they raised their voices together in prayer to God" (Acts 4:24). The report that follows indicates that these Christians, like the Old Testament people of God, prayed together from the Psalms. The communion of the saints is a fellowship of prayer. Spiros Zodhiates has applied this great truth in a practical way:

[I]n prayer *I am not alone*. I am one with the members of God's family, which is also my family. My weak prayer is caught up into the great stream of prayer that goes up forever from God's family. The strength of my prayer is that it is not simply mine; that the moment I fall upon my knees I am no longer an individual man or woman talking to God, but a member of the family of God, a sharer in that human nature which Christ has carried to the right hand of God.

The communion of saints is what gives life and force to prayer, comfort and confidence to those who pray. *On my knees I cannot be alone.* My prayer, as weak, as feeble, as helpless as it is, is organically united with the prayers of the whole Church. We are all members of one body. We belong to an association for intercessory prayer.[5]

Christians "come together" to offer prayers, to listen to the reading and preaching of the Scriptures, and to celebrate the sacraments of baptism and communion. This is how the church has always experienced the communion of the saints. Writing in the second century, Justin Martyr (c. 100–165) preserved the memory of the worship of the postapostolic church:

On the day called Sunday there is a meeting in one place of those who live in cities or the country, and the memoirs of the apostles or the writings of the prophets are read as long as time permits. When the reader has finished, the president in a discourse urges and invites [us] to the imitation of these noble things. Then we all stand up together and offer prayers. And, as said before, when we have finished the prayer, bread is brought, and wine and water, and the president similarly sends up prayers and thanksgivings to the best of his ability, and the congregation assents, saying the Amen; the distribution, and reception of the consecrated [elements] by each one, takes place and they are sent to the absent by the deacons. Those who prosper, and who so wish, contribute, each one as much as he chooses to. What is collected is deposited with the president, and he takes care of orphans and widows, and those who are in want on account of sickness or any other cause, and those who are in bonds, and the strangers who are sojourners among [us], and, briefly, he is the protector of all those in need. We all hold this common gathering on Sunday, since it is the first day, on which God transforming darkness and matter made the universe, and Jesus Christ our Saviour rose from the dead on the same day.[6]

This is the communion of the saints in worship. It sounds very much like the worship of the New Testament church. It also ought to sound like the worship of the contemporary church, for it is the kind of covenant assembly that God has always required.

SEVEN

The Communion Table

The cup of blessing which we bless, is it not the communion of the blood of Christ? The bread which we break, is it not the communion of the body of Christ? For we being many are one bread, and one body: for we are all partakers of that one bread. (1 Cor. 10:16–17 KJV)

Saints, by profession, are bound to maintain an holy fellowship and communion in the worship of God. (Confession of Faith, 26.2)

There is more than one way to say, "I love you." Love can be communicated in tender words. Love can be shared with an affectionate gesture or a warm smile. But love is often most vividly expressed by the presentation of a gift. A photograph, a ring, some perfume, even a greeting card—these are valuable tokens of love.

The Lord Jesus Christ did not leave his saints without tokens of his love. The sacraments of baptism and the Lord's Supper show his union with them and their communion with one another. We have already seen how baptism is a tangible sign of cleansing from sin and new life in Christ (Rom. 6:3–4). Christ also instituted "the communion" as a demonstration of God's love for us (1 Cor. 10:16). Thomas Boston described the Lord's Supper as "a seal of our union and communion with Christ" that "strengthens our union with him."[1] Our fellowship with Christ and with one another is deepened as we see, touch, and taste the bread and the cup.

Why the Lord's Supper Is Called Communion

The ceremony instituted by Christ with bread and the cup has had different names over the centuries. The medieval church called it the Mass. This title was derived from the Latin words at the close of the liturgy—*Ite, missa est*—which meant "Go; it [the meeting] is dismissed." Some Protestants call it the Eucharist, a name that comes from the Greek word used in Luke 22:19 for thanksgiving: *eucharisteo*. Just as Jesus "gave thanks" when he broke bread at the Last Supper (Luke 22:19), so Christians give thanks when they eat their sacramental bread. Others use the name Paul chooses to give in 1 Corinthians 11:20: "the Lord's Supper."

It is also appropriate to call the Lord's Supper "Communion." This title, which is based on 1 Corinthians 10:16, expresses the communal nature of the sacrament. "Communion" is the English translation of the Greek word *koinonia*, which, as we have discovered, has a variety of meanings. Sometimes it means "fellowship," such as the *koinonia* we have with the triune God (1 John 1:3; 2 Cor. 13:14). This fellowship, or *koinonia*, was also a privilege that the saints enjoyed within the New Testament church (Acts 2:42; 1 John 1:3, 7). In other places *koinonia* has the sense of "sharing." Sharing with the poor (Heb. 13:16), showing charity to missionaries (Phil. 4:15), and participating in a collection for needy believers (2 Cor. 8:4) are all ways to demonstrate Christian *koinonia*.

The various uses of the term *koinonia* teach us that the Lord's Supper is something we share. When Jesus Christ instituted Communion, he shared it with all of his disciples (Matt. 26:17–30). The

Book of Acts records that "the breaking of bread" was a customary part of the corporate worship of the early church (Acts 2:42; 20:7). It was not simply a way of sharing a meal together but a way of proclaiming the death and resurrection of Jesus (1 Cor. 11:26). From the beginning, the Lord's Supper was part of communal worship. To put it another way, celebrating Communion is one way to share in the communion of the saints.

The Mode and Meaning of Communion

The Lord's Supper should always be observed according to God's pattern. This includes the faithful preaching of the gospel, so that the sacrament is not separated from the Word; the words of institution, or Christ's invitation for believers to participate (1 Cor. 11:23–26); an exhortation to self-examination, with a warning that unbelievers should not receive the sacrament (1 Cor. 11:27–29); a thanksgiving blessing to consecrate each element (Mark 14:22–23); the breaking and distribution of bread (Matt. 26:26); the appointment and passing of a cup with juice from the vine (Matt. 26:27); and waiting for all to be served before anyone partakes (1 Cor. 11:33). Many churches also take a collection for the poor after the meal, consistent with what may have been the apostles' custom (John 13:29). Perhaps singing a hymn should close every Communion service, as it did at the first observance (Mark 14:26). However, the apostle Paul mentions none of these practices in 1 Corinthians 11:20–34, where we find the plainest teaching concerning the ceremony.

The first time that our Lord Jesus Christ distributed the bread and the cup, he explained their meaning to his disciples. The church long has been divided over what that meaning is. The Protestant Reformation of the sixteenth century witnessed much debate concerning Christ's pronouncement: "This is my body given for you" (Luke

22:19). These have been perhaps the most frequently disputed words in all of Scripture.

Martin Luther believed that the Roman Catholic doctrine called *transubstantiation* was in error. The Catholics taught that in their inward essence the bread and the wine become the flesh and blood of Jesus at their consecration, so that the physical elements become worthy of adoration. This view is partly based on a misunderstanding of Jesus' statement, "My flesh is real food and my blood is real drink" (John 6:55). According to the Catholic interpretation, each time the Mass is celebrated, the real sacrifice of Jesus' death for sin is renewed. Instead of Communion tables, therefore, Roman Catholic churches have stone altars, suitable for making sacrifices. And instead of ministers, they have priests, like the priests who offered sacrifices at the temple. The Roman Catholic Church continues to maintain that those who eat the elements consume part of Christ's dying body and thereby automatically receive sanctification for their sins. The main problem with this view is that Jesus Christ is the only priest we need: "He sacrificed for [our] sins once for all when he offered himself" (Heb. 7:27). No further sacrifice should or even could be offered for sin. We must be careful, therefore, if we refer in the Lord's Supper to "eating Christ's flesh" and "drinking his blood," not to teach that Christ is being sacrificed for sin all over again.

Luther taught the doctrine since known as *consubstantiation*. According to the Lutheran view, the physical body and blood of Christ are "beneath, with, and in" the elements, even though the bread and wine are not transformed. Luther believed that although Christ's body cannot be sensed by taste or sight, there is a physical presence of the crucified body and blood in Communion. He was careful to say, however, that grace is not automatically imparted to those who eat and drink the elements.

Ulrich Zwingli (1484–1531), the early Swiss Reformer, held a position very different from Luther and the Catholics. He and most of the Reformed churches in northern Switzerland and Germany believed that the Lord's Supper was primarily a memorial service that looked back to Christ's sufferings and death on the cross. What was important in Communion was not so much Christ's presence as his absence. Indeed, Christ could not be present in the sacrament because he was risen and ascended to heaven. Zwingli did not believe that Christians could dispense with observing the Supper, but neither did he find in the elements such an actual presence of Christ's person as to impart functional value to them. It was the obedience to Christ's institution that was a means of grace for Zwingli, not Christ's presence in the wine or bread. Zwingli understood the way that the Lord's Supper strengthens the communion of saints. As chaplain of the Swiss army, he often compared Communion with the ceremony in which Swiss soldiers pledged an oath of allegiance to their country. The red cross on their uniforms was the symbol of their solidarity. Similarly, at Communion, Christians take an oath of allegiance to Christ. Communion is the badge of their belonging to Christ and his church.

John Calvin's understanding of the Lord's Supper included doctrinal insights from Luther and Zwingli. Like Luther, he taught that there was a "real presence" of Christ in the Communion. However, Calvin taught that this was a real *spiritual* presence. Although Christ is now in heaven with the Father, he is present in the sacrament by his Holy Spirit. The Lord's Supper imparts grace to participants who truly believe in Christ's promises, but it does not do so by becoming the physical body or blood of Jesus. Rather, God's Holy Spirit dispenses grace through the faith of those who share the bread and the cup.

Like Zwingli, Calvin understood that the Lord's Supper looks back to Christ's sufferings and death. He also recognized that the sacrament is an expression of the communion of saints, a sign and a seal of belonging to Christ's community. He thus described Communion as "a help whereby we may be engrafted into Christ's body, or, engrafted, may grow more and more together with him, until he perfectly joins us with him in the heavenly life."[2] The mention of "heavenly life" is a reminder that the Lord's Supper looks to the future as well as to the past. As Jesus commanded, we proclaim his death "until he comes" (1 Cor. 11:26).

All of this is the work of God's Spirit, who is the bond of our union with Christ and communion with one another. The biblical understanding of the work of the Holy Spirit in Communion is clearly explained in the Heidelberg Catechism:

> [To eat the crucified body and to drink the shed blood of Christ] is not only to embrace with a believing heart all the sufferings and death of Christ, and thereby to obtain the pardon of sin and life eternal; but also, beside that, to become more and more united to His sacred body, by the Holy Ghost, who dwells both in Christ and in us; so that we, although Christ is in heaven and we on earth, are, notwithstanding, "flesh of His flesh and bone of His bone"; and that we live and are governed forever by one Spirit, as members of the same body are by one soul. (Q. & A. 76)

Dangers of the Communion

The Lord's Supper is a solemn ordinance, and there are a number of potential dangers to receiving it. One is unworthy participation, which results in sickness and death. The apostle Paul warns that those who are not worthy to eat and drink the Lord's Supper will eat and drink condemnation unto themselves by not discerning the Lord's body. This is why many of the Corinthians were "weak and sick," and why some had died (1 Cor. 11:30).

Whether a Christian is worthy to take part in the Lord's Table is not easy to determine. The prodigal son said that he was not worthy to participate in the father's household and asked only to be made a servant (Luke 15:19). The Roman military officer who built a synagogue for the Jews considered his house unworthy to entertain Jesus when the Lord came to heal his servant (Luke 7:6). Yet both of these men received grace. What makes us truly worthy is a correct understanding of our unworthiness before God, together with a firm resolve to obey him irrespective of the cost. This is how Calvin summarized the worthiness that God requires:

> [L]et us remember that this sacred feast is medicine for the sick, solace for sinners, alms to the poor; but would bring no benefit to the healthy, righteous, and rich—if such could be found. . . . [T]his is the worthiness—the best and only kind we can bring to God—to offer our vileness and (so to speak) our unworthiness to him so that his mercy may make us worthy of him; to despair in ourselves so that we may be comforted in him . . . moreover, to aspire to that unity which he commends to us in his Supper; and, as he makes all of us one in himself, to desire one soul, one heart, one tongue for us all.[3]

Notice how Calvin concludes: by emphasizing our commitment to be united to all the saints in Christ.

What disqualifies someone from eating the Lord's Supper is willful disregard for its significance (1 Cor. 11:29). Some take part as a matter of courtesy to the minister, as though to decline would be disorderly or rude. Others think that they are earning God's favor by eating and drinking at the table he has spread. Some participate so as not to stand out from the crowd. But people who participate for these reasons should be strongly warned not to take part in the Communion. A wise minister will remind his congregation that the Lord's Table is only for those who "discern the Lord's body" and do not willingly profane it.

Another danger is distraction. Distractions often hinder our experience of corporate worship. When we begin to listen to a sermon, or to think about the words of a hymn we are singing, or to focus on the words of a public prayer, our minds are tempted to run astray. So too when we observe the Lord's Supper. No doubt there are spiritual enemies at work to starve our souls of the spiritual nourishment we may receive at the Lord's Table (Eph. 6:11–12).

One reason we find it difficult to worship is that Satan and his demons know that our worship at the Lord's Table advances our communion with God and with one another. We need to fight valiantly to govern our thoughts and to avoid distractions in our obedience to his gracious invitation. Our Lord wants us to be attentive during Communion. He established the Lord's Table as an ordinance for the gathered saints. Our bodies are insensitive to spiritual exercises. If we are not well rested we may get tired and sleepy. We may become disturbed by the physical presence of our neighbors. But we must not allow these things to distract our souls from the important business of spiritual worship.

Blessings of the Communion

Does the Lord's Supper promote our fellowship and communion with fellow Christians? If it does not, we have misunderstood it or have allowed it to become a meaningless ritual. Walter Chantry once observed that "in modern times, evangelicals wrongly think that the best, the real fellowship takes place apart from formal worship. Actually, prayer together, hearing the word together, hymns sung together are the richest God-appointed activities of fellowship."

The sacraments belong in any list of worship components that promote our communion. The Confession of Faith states, "Saints, by profession, are bound to maintain an holy fellowship and communion in the worship of God, and in performing such other spiritual services as tend to their mutual edification" (26.2). The Lord's Supper encourages this spiritual communion, first by focusing our worship on the new testament through Christ's blood. The reason we may eat common bread and drink a common cup is because we benefit from one and the same covenant between our Lord Jesus and his Father. In legal terms, we are third-party beneficiaries to the contract. We gave nothing of value to participate, nor were we consulted before the agreement was made. But our heavenly Father has sent his divine Son to save a whole world of sinners, his elect people, by paying the penalty due for their sin. The symbol of Christ's body and blood evidences a last will and testament in which Christ Jesus designated us as the heirs of his inheritance.

When a rich man dies, frequently his heirs gather at a memorial service. Family members should not focus on the cash bequests but on the spiritual legacy of the one who has died. Perhaps the importance or virtue of his life will be the subject of a testimony. Perhaps the love he had for his family will be discussed, or even his manner of death. Similar reflections are appropriate parts of the Communion. We should use the Lord's Supper to remember Christ's painful and embarrassing death. This will draw us closer to him and consequently closer to his loved ones. Further, we should remember the fruits of that death. He paid the penalty due for our sins. His blood was spilled on the ground, and his body suffered real agony of torture. What better memory device could point us to the reality of hell? Any who think lightly of sin need only linger at the Communion table and consider the price that Jesus paid for it.

The Lord's Supper also encourages spiritual communion by reminding us of the possibility of betrayal. Friends may betray us. Paul told the Corinthians that the Lord's Supper was established on the same night that Jesus was betrayed (1 Cor. 11:23). When Judas Iscariot was revealed to be a traitor, the eleven apostles must have been surprised. Participants at the Lord's Table should be aware of the unreliability of fellow disciples. Even church leaders may fall into scandalous sin (Acts 20:30). Yet the supper reminds us that if our friends are unfaithful, Christ himself experienced such infidelity.

To illustrate what Christ's example means for the communion of the saints, consider what happened during the celebration of the Lord's Supper at a little mission church in New Zealand:

> A line of worshipers had just knelt at the altar rail when suddenly from among them a young native arose and returned to his pew. Some minutes later, however, he returned to his place at the rail. Afterward a friend inquired why he had done this, and he replied, "When I went forward and knelt, I found myself side by side with a man who some years ago had slain my father and whom I had vowed to kill. I felt I could not partake with him, so I returned to my pew. But as I sat there, my mind went back to a picture of the Upper Room, with its table set, and I heard a voice saying, 'By this shall all men know that ye are my disciples, if ye have love one to another.' And then I saw a Cross with a man nailed upon it and the same voice saying, 'Father, forgive them for they know not what they do.' It was then I arose and returned to the altar rail."[4]

There is also the possibility that we may betray others. Before we commune we must examine our hearts. Are we more interested in money than in the honor and glory of Christ? Do we care enough to speak after the service to those eating bread next to us? Perhaps they are in the jaws of temptation to depart from the fellowship. Do we notice absent church members as well as those present? Will we visit them to let them know that they are missed? These questions remind us to be faithful to all the saints and not to betray them.

The Lord's Supper renews our commitment to our faithful friends within the body of Christ, notwithstanding disappointment or betrayal by others. Husbands or wives may leave us, even if they profess to be disciples of the Lord. Christian employers or coworkers may let us down. But God will remain faithful forever. "When my father and my mother forsake me," David sang, "then the LORD will take me up" (Ps. 27:10 KJV). He has told us to continue fellowship with fellow Christians, no matter how great the discouragement due to unfaithful friends. By persisting in gathering around the Lord's Table we confirm our faith that he is coming again to correct all injustices, even those (or perhaps especially those) within the church.

Finally, the Lord's Supper encourages spiritual communion by breaking down social and class barriers. The apostle Paul taught that the Lord's Supper must not insult or exclude the poor by the manner of its observance (1 Cor. 11:22). One social class in the Corinthian church had prepared expensive meals for the Lord's Table. Some became drunk with an abundance of wine, while others left the common table hungry (1 Cor. 11:21). The rich were invited to a table with fine wine and expensive bread, while the social outcasts had to sit at another table to drink what was left over. This practice undercut all fellowship, respect, and mutual love. Paul told them to wait until everyone was served before anyone began the ceremony of eating and drinking, and to eat and drink together (1 Cor. 11:33).

In modern observance of the Communion, there is hardly any danger of getting drunk from the beverage served. However, do we try to sit next to strangers at the service rather than with our close friends? Do we ask those who may not participate in the Lord's Supper if they want us to pray for them? If strangers participate, do we ask them following the service to share their personal testimony? There is nothing unrighteous about seeking solitude after the Lord's Supper to deal with conviction of sin. And, of course, Communion is no time to stare across the congregation or to be a busybody. However, we must be conscious of those around us. We should use the service to minister to their needs with words of inquiry and encouragement.

Jesus could have assigned special significance to a private meal, but the Lord's Table is a family table. The saints who commune are all members of one family, and the table spread with bread and wine is for the entire family. This fellowship consists of people with light skin and dark, rich and poor, men and women, young and old—we are all one in Christ (Gal. 3:26–28).

Hughes Oliphant Old tells a beautiful story about experiencing the communion of the saints. The story deserves to be told in full:

> It was Christmas of 1969 and I was a student in Germany. I had gone to spend the Christmas vacation in the Benedictine monastery of Maria Laach hidden away in the Eifel forest behind Koblenz. It was a beautiful place, a perfectly preserved Romanesque monastery where monks had maintained the singing of their daily office for something like a thousand years. There was this monastery beside a crater lake surrounded by a hemlock forest. What an inspiration!
>
> Soon after I arrived I met another guest in the monastery, a student from Romania. He had left his young wife and their infant son in Romania so that he could come to the University of Freiburg and study the Bible. But no one in Freiburg wanted to teach him the Bible. I told him I would teach him the Bible, and with that he gave me a bear hug. For the rest of the vacation we studied the Bible, walking in the forest all day, every day. He had his Romanian Bible, I had my English Bible, and we discussed it in German.
>
> After supper on Christmas Eve there was a knock at my door. One of the monks had been sent to remind me that as a Protestant minister I should not present myself for communion on Christmas morning. He was, to be sure, very polite about it. That was no problem for me; I understood those were the rules.

The next morning after prayers I left the chapel and walked out in the snow with my new friend Joan. He was terribly upset. He too had been told that he could not receive communion because he was Romanian Orthodox. He took me by the hand very forcefully and said, "While they are having their Christmas Mass here let's go for a walk around the lake." Having been brought up under communism he did not know much Bible, and so he had me go over the Christmas story.

An hour later, after I had told him all I could think of about the birth of Christ, we arrived at a little chapel directly across the lake from the monastery. My friend wanted to go in to pray. Once inside he pulled out of his pocket a breakfast roll and half a bottle of wine and said to me, "You're a Protestant priest. I am your congregation. We must celebrate the feast." So, we did. As we read our German Bible together and I tried to say the communion prayers in German, slowly it began to dawn on me, What could glorify God more? Here were two young men, one from the communist world, one from the capitalist world, united together in the communion of saints. This little supper fulfilled one of the promises of Jesus Christ: "I say to you that many will come from the east and the west, and will take their places at the feast with Abraham, Isaac, and Jacob in the kingdom of heaven" (Matt. 8:11).

In the gathering of this global feast we taste God's glory.

EIGHT

Gifts and Graces

*But to each one of us grace has been given as Christ apportioned it.
. . . It was he who gave some to be apostles, some to be prophets,
some to be evangelists, and some to be pastors and teachers, to prepare God's people for works of service, so that the body of Christ may
be built up until we all reach unity in the faith and in the knowledge
of the Son of God and become mature, attaining to the whole measure of the fullness of Christ. (Eph. 4:7, 11–13)*

*All saints, that are united to Jesus Christ . . . and united to one an-
other in love . . . have communion in each other's gifts and graces.
(Confession of Faith, 26.1)*

Early in his journey, the man named Christian in John Bunyan's timeless allegory *Pilgrim's Progress* stumbles into a swamp of despair. He is deserted by his companion—a man named Pliable, suitably enough—and struggles to continue his journey forward through the quicksand of discouragement. The only way he is able finally to gain a footing on solid ground is through the uplifting hand of a newfound friend named Help.[1] Bunyan uses this picture to teach us that we need (and will find) help along our pilgrimage of faith. And there is another lesson from this incident: the help may come from us, and the pilgrim may turn out to be another believer who needs our assistance.

There are many ways to help other Christians. As we shall discover in chapter 9, one way to express our communion is by providing financial support for our fellow saints. But we must also share the spiritual gifts and graces that the Lord has donated to his people: "To each one the manifestation of the Spirit is given for the common good" (1 Cor. 12:7). In his commentary on the Heidelberg Catechism, George Bethune wrote:

> It is the order of grace that Christians are instrumentally dependent upon each other; as we grow they grow; and as they grow we grow. Whatever we do for their benefit is for our own; whatever they do for our benefit is for their own. Thus it is not only our duty, but our best interest, to impart freely of all God's gifts to us for the benefit of our fellow-Christians. There must be a communion of prayers and acts and gifts, as there is a communion of grace. If we refuse this closeness of union to our fellow-Christians, we shall suffer doubly; for the Holy Spirit will not use us as the channels of his grace to them, nor can the effectual working through them reach us. Nothing but weakness and death can result from such selfish isolation.[2]

The Bible contains many examples of believers who depended on the help of other believers. Moses was given the seventy elders of Israel to assist him in governing the Israelites (Num. 11:17). Only in error did Elijah believe that he had been left alone to withstand the idolatry of Jezebel and the prophets of Baal (1 Kings 19:10, 18). The apostle Paul used his gifts primarily to benefit others (1 Cor. 10:33). Paul in turn depended on the generosity and hard work of his many partners in the gospel. The slave Onesimus willingly used his gifts and graces first for Paul and then for his earthly superior, Philemon

(Philem. 10–14). We are told to act the same way, looking not only to our interests but also to the interests of others (Phil. 2:4).

Why Gifts and Graces Are Given

The Westminster Confession of Faith speaks of the saints having "communion in each other's gifts and graces" (26.1). Both gifts and graces are loans to the church from God's unconditional kindness. By graces, the Westminster Divines meant attitudes and dispositions rather than specific talents. A grace is a Christian virtue that, as the word implies, is donated by God's unmerited favor. Spiritual gifts, however, are those benefits of God's favor that equip the saints to accomplish specific tasks. A gift is "a capacity for service which is given to every true Christian without exception and which is something each did not possess before he became a Christian."[3]

Each member's spiritual gifts and graces are bestowed to benefit the whole body, "to prepare God's people for works of service, so that the body of Christ may be built up" (Eph. 4:12). To achieve this goal, every Christian has one or more gifts. As Zacharias Ursinus explained it, the gifts of the body are "so distributed to all its members that some excel in one particular kind of gift, whilst others again excel in other respects; for there are different gifts of the Spirit, and 'to every one of us is given grace, according to the measure of the gift of Christ' (Eph. 4:7)."[4]

Some spiritual gifts are closely related to natural talents. Although a gift is different from a talent, some gifts can be expressed through a talent. For example, a Christian may exercise the gift of helping through baking, carpentry, or some other practical skill. Or a man may express his talent for public speaking through the gift of preaching. The main distinction between natural talents and true spiritual gifts is that the gifts of the Spirit are only for Christians, and they are only to be used for a spiritual purpose.

Gifts are also closely related to graces. In Ephesians 4:7 the apostle Paul uses the word *grace* to refer to what are spiritual gifts. (This alerts us that the Confession of Faith may use the term *grace* somewhat differently than the apostle.) Similarly in 1 Corinthians 12 and 13 Paul freely moves from a discussion of spiritual gifts to a discussion of the graces of faith, hope, and love. Our gifts are entrusted to us by grace, and our graces equip us to exercise our gifts. Both are to be used for the benefit of others.

Christ gives spiritual gifts and graces to adorn and equip the church for the work it is called to do. Some graces make the saints more beautiful, like humility, patience, and self-control. Others are more utilitarian, such as faith, generosity, and goodness. But God grants all his gifts and graces for the benefit of his entire body, and all are necessary for the advancement of his kingdom: "The body is a unit, though it is made up of many parts; and though all its parts are many, they form one body. . . . Now you are the body of Christ, and each one of you is a part of it" (1 Cor. 12:12, 27).

The purpose of God's giving gifts and graces is communal, not personal. My spiritual gifts are not my own; they belong to Christ and to his church. This is of the essence of the communion of the saints. In answer to the question, "What do you understand by 'the communion of saints'?" the Heidelberg Catechism gives this answer: "First, that all and every one who believes, being members of Christ, are in common partakers of him, and of all his riches and gifts; secondly, that every one must know it to be his duty, readily and cheerfully to employ his gifts for the advantage and salvation of other members" (Q. & A. 55).

This answer reminds us that the communion of the saints flows from our communion in Christ. Jesus used the metaphor of a branch in a vine to describe this communion (John 15:1–8). The branch can bear fruit only for as long as it is connected to the vine; when it is cut off, it is no longer useful. Jesus—the true vine—is the source of all gifts and graces. To extend the metaphor, a branch benefits from other parts of the vine as well, like its leaves, runners, and bark. Only a vine with many branches is very fruitful. In the communion of the saints, God has established a vine with many branches, as well as leaves and fruit. Suppose a cluster of grapes should despise its leaves? The fruit would not be able gather sunlight and grow sweeter. If a branch left the vine it would soon wither and die because the moisture gathered by roots from the earth could not reach it. Even so, a Christian cut off from the fellowship of the saints and separated from the fellowship of the whole body of Christ will become stunted and virtually lifeless.

The communion of saints is advanced through the work of the Holy Spirit. Though deeds of charity, words of encouragement, and times of social interaction are necessary, Christian community is essentially spiritual, not social. It centers on the worship of God, which requires the exercise of the whole body's spiritual gifts. Those with musical talents will lead the singing. Those who can teach will do so. Those who can explain and apply the Word of God will preach. Those entrusted with gifts and graces for mercy will offer material assistance. We have a diversity of gifts so that we can all make some contribution to the work of the body, while we all depend on one and the same God: "There are different kinds of gifts, but the same Spirit. There are different kinds of service, but the same Lord. There are different kinds of working, but the same God works all of them in all men" (1 Cor. 12:4–6).

What Are God's Gifts and Graces?

In the early church spiritual gifts included miracles such as the ability to cast out evil spirits (Acts 19:11–12), speaking in unknown tongues (Acts 2:4–6), supernatural healing (1 Cor. 12:9–10), and even raising the dead back to life (Acts 20:9–12). These extraordinary gifts were given to edify the church by confirming the truth of the apostolic gospel (1 Cor. 14:26; Heb. 2:4). The gifts given to the early church also included extraordinary callings such as apostle and prophet (Eph. 4:11; 1 Cor. 12:28).

In our day we share what might be called ordinary gifts, though these are no less valuable than the extraordinary gifts of the apostles. Teaching (Rom. 12:7; 1 Tim. 3:2), evangelism (Eph. 4:11), preaching (1 Tim. 4:13–14), governing (1 Tim. 5:17), helping (1 Cor. 12:28), singleness (Matt. 19:12; 1 Cor. 7:7–8), faith (1 Cor. 12:9), and discernment (Acts 23:6; 1 John 4:1) are among the ordinary gifts that now flourish within the communion of the saints. The New Testament lists the various gifts of the Spirit in five different places (see Eph. 4:11; 1 Cor. 12:8–10, 28–30; Rom. 12:6–8; 1 Peter 4:11). Although there is some overlap, no two lists are the same, which means that all the lists must be studied to gain a complete understanding of spiritual gifts.

Although these gifts are called "spiritual," they are not the product of the third person of the Trinity alone. Spiritual gifts also come from the heavenly Father (James 1:17) and from the Lord Jesus Christ (Eph. 4:7). The triune God dispenses gifts and graces among his people as he desires. The principal means for obtaining spiritual gifts are personal desire (1 Cor. 12:31) and prayerful petition (Matt. 7:11), together with thanksgiving for what we have already been given (Phil. 4:6).

The New Testament also lists many spiritual graces, those virtuous dispositions that adorn the Christian life. Some of the most well-known spiritual graces are described as "the fruit of the Spirit: love, joy, peace, patience, kindness, goodness, faithfulness, gentleness and self-control" (Gal. 5:22). However, the Spirit's graces also include compassion and humility (1 Peter 3:8), a forgiving spirit (Col. 3:13), hope (Rom. 5:5), mercy (Col. 3:12), sincerity (Rom. 12:9), impartiality (James 2:1), thankfulness (Heb. 13:15), generosity (2 Cor. 9:7), hospitality (Heb. 13:2), fervency (Rom. 12:11), and many other spiritual virtues mentioned throughout the Scriptures. Each one of these graces is for every believer, although not every believer has every grace in equal measure.

Sometimes the church's treasure is a gift and a grace. For example, generosity is a grace shared by rich and poor alike, even though from a financial standpoint, those who are destitute may not excel in the amount they give. It is a privilege to be able to give (Acts 20:35). However, some will have to share in the gift of giving that God has bestowed upon others. For this reason, donations of money should not be public displays (Matt. 6:2–4) but private collections turned over to leaders of the church for distribution in the name of the whole communion of saints (1 Cor. 16:1–3). In this way, even poorer members of a congregation will be able to take part in large gifts. What is important is that everyone should give something (Mark 12:42–43).

Any two or three spiritual gifts would be insufficient on their own. We must be complete in every good work, and for that reason we must share in each other's gifts and graces. We cannot all exhibit all of the Spirit's fruit all of the time. So, for example, when one believer's faith runs low, another believer's faith lends needed help. When one is healed, others benefit from the Lord's mercy (see Phil. 2:27). And when one believer excels in hospitality, that gracious gift benefits the whole body. As Clement of Rome (c. A.D.100) wrote in his first epistle to the Corinthians,

> Let our whole body, then, be preserved in Christ Jesus; and let every one be subject to his neighbour, according to the special gift bestowed upon him. Let the strong not despise the weak, and let the weak show respect unto the strong. Let the rich man provide for the wants of the poor; and let the poor man bless God, because He hath given him one by whom his need may be supplied.[5]

The Things That Divide

God intends his gifts and graces to unite the saints, bringing harmony out of their diversity. As Paul explained to the Corinthians, "God has combined the members of the body and has given greater honor to the parts that lacked it, so that there should be no division in the body, but that its parts should have equal concern for each other" (1 Cor. 12:24–25). Yet sometimes gifts and graces turn out to be the things that divide the saints, which was Paul's concern. Spiritual gifts can become a source of pride or resentment, with the result that the unity of the body is disturbed.

Perhaps this a good place to distinguish among three common obstacles to Christian community: error, heresy, and schism. *Error* is any deviation in belief or practice from the truth contained in the Bible. *Heresy* is a denial of any biblical truth that is essential to believe for salvation. *Schism* is division within the communion of saints caused when human demands are made prerequisites for fellowship.

Not every doctrinal error is heresy. Furthermore, not every member of a church that tolerates heresy necessarily believes its damnable doctrines. Errors that do not amount to heresy can nonetheless interfere with the communion of the saints. Wrong views of the role of church leaders, misunderstandings concerning the sacraments, and arguments about creeds and confessions often divide the body of Christ. We need to be careful not to condemn those whom God accepts. Unless a doctrinal mistake concerns an essential element of the Christian faith or a person's misconduct is scandalous (1 Cor. 5:11), we should not exclude a fellow pilgrim from our fellowship.

Realize that every Christian unknowingly participates in some error, either in doctrine or in practice. If we did not, we would be ready for heaven. Since God wants us to live in harmony in the church, we must accept some whom we believe to be in error. This causes weak Christians difficulty because they think it requires compromise, which many view as the worst sin of all. However, accepting the gifts and graces of a brother or sister who is in error does not constitute compromise, nor does it require that we change our views. The Scripture commands us to "accept him whose faith is weak, without passing judgment on disputable matters" (Rom. 14:1).

Strictly speaking, heresy cannot divide the communion of saints because, by definition, heretics are not rightly part of the church: "Warn a divisive person once, and then warn him a second time. After that have nothing to do with him. You may be sure that such a man is warped and sinful; he is self-condemned" (Titus 3:10–11). Nevertheless we should not be surprised to encounter heresy in the church. God sometimes allows a heresy to develop in order plainly to segregate the truth from error. But we do need to guard ourselves and others from falling into heresy and thereby falling into ruin.

Schism does not necessarily involve either heresy or error. Even though a group of Christians may hold to correct doctrine, they can be schismatic toward other saints if they impose standards that go beyond Scripture. Schism is segregation from Christians who look, believe, or behave differently. Sometimes schism results in the formation of new churches or denominations. It includes racial segregation among believers, as well as separation from fellow saints in attitude or geography.

Schism is nearly always the result of sin. Yet on occasion God glorifies himself through the separation of true believers. A good example is Paul and Barnabas, who had a sharp disagreement concerning the young evangelist, John Mark (Acts 15:39). Paul had such deep mistrust of Mark that he separated from Barnabas, who insisted on giving the young man another chance to prove himself. This division was not what either Paul or Barnabas judged best at the time, but it proved to be necessary, and God used it to accomplish his good purpose in the end (see 2 Tim. 4:11).

Notwithstanding God's ability to use schism for the ultimate good of his people, it is an evil to be avoided because it compromises our witness to the world. That is why Paul urged the women who were fighting in the church at Philippi to mend their differences—"to agree with each other in the Lord," as he put it (Phil. 4:2). It is also why he criticized the church at Corinth for its many divisions and appealed to them "in the name of our Lord Jesus Christ, that all of you agree with one another so that there may be no divisions among you and that you may be perfectly united in mind and thought" (1 Cor. 1:10). Christ wants his people to be united in love so that we can display the unity of God to the world (John 17:21).

Finding and Using Your Gifts and Graces

While we must not be naïve about the possibility of division, we must also embrace the joys of sharing in one another's gifts and graces. Paul reminded the Ephesians that "from him [Christ] the whole body, joined and held together by every supporting ligament, grows and builds itself up in love, as each part does its work" (Eph. 4:16). The Puritan John Owen described this verse as "the greatest and most glorious description of the communion of the saints that we have in the Scripture."[6] However, in order for it to become a reality, each saint must know how to do his part. Toward that end, this chapter closes with a few practical suggestions for identifying and exercising spiritual gifts and graces for the cause of Christ (see also the Spiritual Gifts Questionnaire in the appendix).

The place to begin is by considering what gifts and graces God has granted to us. Once we understand what the Bible has to say about spiritual gifts, we should pray for God's guidance. This will protect us from seeking a gift that gratifies our desires but that God does not intend to give us. Alternatively, we may at first be resistant to a gift that God has already given. Yet through prayer we surrender our will to God's will, asking God to use our gifts and graces for his glory.

The next step is to assess our spiritual abilities. In a pamphlet entitled "Finding Your Gift," James Montgomery Boice observed that

> we will be helped by making a sober assessment of our own spiritual strengths and abilities. If we do not do this on the basis of a careful study of the Word of God and through prayer, we will be misled. But if we have first sought the wisdom and mind of God, we can then go back and look at ourselves through spiritual eyes. We can ask: What do I like to do? What am I good at? What are my talents? As we saw earlier, spiritual gifts are not talents. But they are often related, and we are seldom wrong if we try to exercise our talents spiritually and for spiritual ends.

The last step is to seek the wisdom of other Christians. The call to exercise spiritual gifts comes from God, but ordinarily it comes through the church, where our ardor to exercise our gifts is governed by the order of divinely ordained spiritual authority. Often a gift is first exercised in response to a spiritual or practical need in the church. To help match each member to a ministry, an inventory of spiritual gifts should be taken corporately and individually. Leaders of each local church may wish to conduct a spiritual inventory on a regular basis. A new member self-assessment questionnaire may be a useful starting point for carrying on this work. (See the Spiritual Gifts Questionnaire in the appendix.) Furthermore, each of us regularly should make an honest assessment of our talents and abilities and volunteer for the ministry we believe God has equipped us to perform.

Periodic reassessment of spiritual gifts also has salutary effects in the church. A true spiritual gift will not be lost by excessive use, but it does need refreshment, or else it will wither and die. Perhaps a gift or grace has burned out through lack of resupply. In the same way that we blink our eyes so that we can keep on reading or change our shoes so that we can keep on walking, spiritual gifts need to be renewed so that we can keep on serving.

When we consider how to profit from one another's gifts and graces, we sometimes overlook the greatest resource God has given to us: the Christian family. Eve was created and brought to Adam to be a help suited to his needs (Gen. 2:20–22). She was to be a practical and a spiritual encouragement to him. Husbands and wives need the gifts and graces of their spouses. It is the wife's privilege—and should be her joy—to demonstrate the submissive love of Christ as she helps her husband. At the same time, her husband is to use his gifts and graces for her sanctification. It is the husband's privilege—and ought to be his joy—to demonstrate the sacrificial love of Christ as he serves his wife. Children are also entrusted with spiritual gifts and graces. They should seek to grow in the graces and gifts that their parents display, but they should also seek to cultivate gifts and graces of their own. Parents should attempt to learn spiritual lessons from their children and daily teach them the ways of the Lord (Deut. 6:6–7).

The one family that is certain to possess the gifts and graces of the Holy Spirit is the local church. God has chosen to distribute his spiritual gifts and graces through local assemblies. He brings together rich and poor, young and old, men and women, schooled and unschooled so that all might bring glory to Christ: "The body is a unit, though it is made up of many parts; and though all its parts are many, they form one body. So it is with Christ" (1 Cor. 12:12). Each part of the body has a task to accomplish. Not all of these duties are glamorous, but even the ordinary functions of the body are necessary. No believer should despise his or her spiritual gifts because they seem less important. One Christian may be a gifted preacher. Another may play the piano or organ to assist in congregational singing. Someone else has the talent to care for the church's plumbing or electrical system.

Still another may be good with arithmetic and have discernment in financial matters. Each is necessary, and each is honorable.

Since we have different gifts, it is sometimes tempting to exalt our gifts and denigrate the gifts of others, as if what we do for Christ is somehow more important than what others do. May God grant to us the humility to appreciate his gifts to others and the grace to share our own spiritual gifts as widely as we can: "If anyone speaks, he should do it as one speaking the very words of God. If anyone serves, he should do it with the strength God provides, so that in all things God may be praised through Jesus Christ. To him be the glory and the power for ever and ever. Amen" (1 Peter 4:11).

Relief in Outward Things

All the believers were together and had everything in common.
Selling their possessions and goods, they gave to anyone
as he had need. (Acts 2:44–45)

Saints by profession are bound . . . also in relieving each other in out-
ward things, according to their several abilities and necessities.
(Confession of Faith, 26.2)

To love God is to love others, and to love others is to love God. These
two loves cannot be separated. When an expert in the law asked Jesus
to identify the greatest commandment in the law, he replied: " 'Love
the Lord your God with all your heart and with all your soul and with
all your mind.' This is the first and greatest commandment" (Matt.
22:37–38). But Jesus was not content to let that answer stand on its
own. Immediately he went on to say, "And the second is like it: 'Love
your neighbor as yourself' " (Matt. 22:39).

To love God is to have compassion for the needs of others. In a
popular song called "Love One Another," Steve Green explains that
this compassion will cause the world to "watch in wonder," helping
people understand the nature of Christian love and ultimately trans-

forming the world. "Love one another and your love will change the world."

The idea that Christian love will change the world is biblical. Jesus prayed that his disciples would teach the world about the love of God the Father: "May they be brought to complete unity to let the world know that you sent me and have loved them even as you have loved me" (John 17:23).

The trouble is that many Christians view serving others as an optional extra in the Christian life. Some are preoccupied with satisfying their own needs and gratifying their own desires. Others would rather study the doctrines of the faith than put them into practice by helping their brothers and sisters. As John Calvin warned the citizens of Geneva, when you "show great devotion in the worshipping and serving of him [God], you must not be careless to live justly and uprightly with your neighbors."[1] The truth is that sharing is a Christian duty. Jerry Bridges urges, "We must wean ourselves from the attitude that giving to those in need is something that we may or may not do, depending on our feelings. The issue is not whether to give but rather what needs, of all those that come to our attention, we should respond to."[2] However, because of the special grace that has brought us into the communion of the saints, sharing is not merely a duty but also a joyful response of the heart.

The Confession of Faith encourages the saints to "maintain . . . communion in relieving each other in outward things, according to their several abilities and necessities" (26.2). The standard is not only to love our neighbor but also to strive to maintain the unity of the body of Christ, into which we have been drawn by God's saving grace. Unless we are helping to relieve our brother's material needs, we are not maintaining our communion with the saints. Relief in outward things is not voluntary. It is a manifestation of God's grace in our lives, and it is central to God's plan for saving the world through Jesus Christ.

How Do You Spell Relief?

It is necessary first to dispose of the false notions that grip the Christian community when the theme of relief is mentioned. First, relief in outward things is not a handout for those who display irresponsible behavior in handling the resources that God has entrusted to them. Such actions, if supported by relief, may encourage some to refuse to work and to accept responsibility for themselves and their families. This is often a weakness in government welfare programs. When the same thing is allowed to happen in the church, it can even discredit the gospel, which is why Paul told the Thessalonians, "If a man will not work, he shall not eat" (2 Thess. 3:10). On the contrary, "He who has been stealing must steal no longer, but must work, doing something useful with his own hands, that he may have something to share with those in need" (Eph. 4:28).

Second, Christians are not to give to agencies (the state, secular charities, or even to Christian organizations) who help the needy in order to free themselves from the obligation to help others. The rich biblical term *charity* has become synonymous with writing a check, but genuine charity extends the compassion of Christ to people's deepest needs. And their deepest needs are always spiritual needs, which means that genuine relief demands personal involvement. The church officers who are most directly charged and invested with the duties of mercy are the deacons. However, even though the deacons are to lead the church in service, meeting material needs is the responsibility of individual Christians. God does not intend for deacons to do all the work but for them to help prepare all God's people for deeds of mercy. According to C. Van Dam, "Deacons are those who see to it that there are no forgotten or neglected people in the church of God." They are also the ones "who protect the communal joy of the congregation, and who, therefore, see to it that the exercising of the communion of saints, with all that that implies, continues."[3]

Finally, relief in outward things does not mean that God wants Christians to become communists. As the Confession of Faith puts it, "Nor doth their communion one with another, as saints, take away, or infringe the title or propriety which each man hath in his goods and possessions" (26.3). The example of the Jerusalem church, in which "all the believers were together and had everything in common" (Acts 2:44), has sometimes been misunderstood to demand Christian socialism. True, the first Christians displayed a type of generosity rarely seen in the church today: "Selling their possessions and goods, they gave to anyone as he had need" (Acts 2:45). But even holding "everything in common" does not mean ceasing to hold private property. Some of the first Christians sold their property from time to time (Acts 4:34), but this was done on a voluntary basis. In fact, just a few chapters later Peter insisted that Ananias had the right to keep his property, saying, "Didn't it belong to you before it was sold? And after it was sold, wasn't the money at your disposal?" (Acts 5:4). Relief in outward things demands neither coercive communism nor consumptive capitalism but compassionate *koinonia*.

Koinonia Revisited

If there is a biblical command to assist our brothers and sisters with material needs, how does this command relate to the communion of the saints? We will examine this principle by exploring the biblical term *koinonia*, by searching the Scriptures of the Old and New Testaments to see what the whole Bible teaches about charity, and by noting examples of Christians who have practiced it since the time of Christ.

It is no accident that the biblical term *koinonia* keeps reappearing in this book; it is a rich term. Regrettably, contemporary Christians often limit fellowship to social interaction, sometimes, they hope, involving food and drink. These may be important elements in strengthening the body, but to New Testament Christians the term meant far more. As we have noted previously, *koinonia* is often translated as "sharing," especially as it relates to one's possessions. For example, we are commanded to "share with God's people who are in need" (Rom. 12:13). Sharing with others is the kind of sacrifice that pleases God (Heb. 13:16). Christians in Macedonia and Achaia were happy "to make a contribution for the poor among the saints in Jerusalem" (Rom. 15:26–27). In fact, they "urgently pleaded with us for the privilege of sharing in this service to the saints" (2 Cor. 8:4). Such service is praiseworthy. As Paul went on to say to the Corinthians, "Because of the service by which you have proved yourselves, men will praise God for the obedience that accompanies your confession of the gospel of Christ, and for your generosity in sharing with them and with everyone else" (2 Cor. 9:13). The term *koinonia* occurs in each of these verses. And in each case, sharing with those in need serves to strengthen the communion of the saints. Considered in this light, *koinonia* involves not only belonging to the Christian community but also having an obligation to care for its other members.

When we study the Scriptures to see what the whole Bible teaches about relief in outward things, we immediately realize that the needs of others have always been special to God's heart. God desired his covenant community to share his concern for people's material needs. The first four of the Ten Commandments speak of our obligation to worship God properly (Exod. 20:1–11); the latter six commandments speak of our obligation to value, respect, and ultimately love our neighbor (Exod. 20:12–17). Similarly Jesus reminds us that we are to do for others what we would have them do for us. Doubtless if we were in material need, we would desire others to help us! Therefore we should do the same for others.

It is impossible to read the Old Testament without recognizing

God's compassion for the poor. God gave many specific instructions to Israel for the care of the economically disadvantaged. Farmers were commanded to leave their land unplowed during the seventh year so that "the poor among your people may get food from it" (Exod. 23:11). They were also forbidden from reaping to the edges of their field or gathering the gleanings from their harvest. This was the practice that enabled Ruth to gather barley behind the harvesters in the field of Boaz (Ruth 2). The poor were given reduced rates for guilt offerings: one lamb instead of three (Lev. 14). Provision was made for the poor (Exod. 23:11; Lev. 14:21; 19:10), while special blessings were promised for those who attended to their needs (Ps. 41:1; Prov. 14:12). To mistreat the poor was tantamount to mistreating God (Prov. 17:5). One of the ways the Israelites reminded themselves of their obligations to the poor was by singing about them (Ps. 10:2; 41:1). God knew that the poor would always be with us, which is why he gave his people a perpetual duty to attend to their needs.

Israel often failed to keep these commands. Some of the Bible's strongest words of judgment are reserved for those who took advantage of the poor. The prophets condemned Israel for selling the poor for a pair of shoes (Amos 2:6), for crushing them (Amos 4:1), and even for rejoicing in their destruction (Hab. 3:14). God clearly commanded Israel to provide for the needy, and the exile was God's judgment for their failure to be obedient. In the exile Israel was thus torn from its homeland as a visible lesson that the people had fractured the body by not giving relief to the weak, the needy, and the helpless. Apart from the remnant who would return, the nation of Israel failed to act with compassion. In the life of Israel, therefore, we see the consequences of failing to heed the mandate to help the needy. By failing to obey God's command to help those who were suffering, Israel's unity and fellowship were broken. God's people failed to maintain the true communion of the saints.

A Stern Warning

Are these principles still operative in the New Testament? Can we assume that since we are not under the law but under grace, the consequences of failing to provide relief in outward things are now less serious? Absolutely not. We find instead that whereas in the Old Testament God dealt with his people through Israel, in the New Testament God deals with believers through his church. But in both cases, the common denominator is personal responsibility to care for the needy.

Important teaching about individual accountability appears in Matthew 25:31–46, where Jesus appears upon his throne with his angels to separate the sheep from the goats. The context for this passage is the time "when the Son of Man comes in his glory" (Matt. 25:31). At this final judgment the works of the obedient are clearly distinguished from the acts of the unrighteous. Whereas the obedient exhibit self-denial, contempt of this world, and love for the brethren, sinners reveal a selfish and pleasure-oriented view of life. Jesus illustrates the practices of the obedient: supplying food for the hungry, clothing the naked, giving shelter to the homeless, and offering companionship to the lonely. Those he does not receive into his kingdom are rejected because they failed to assist the sick, the stranger, the naked, and the thirsty. It is by these works that Christ recognizes his own. Even the unrighteous may have some good deeds to offer to Christ, but these works were not offered to "one of the least," and thus they were not done for God's glory.

Jesus did not teach that one's deeds determine one's entrance into the kingdom of God. No work merits eternal life. But the faith of those who have been justified by faith must express itself through love (see Gal. 5:6b). For the true believer, faith is more than an intellectual acknowledgement of the truth. Even the demons believe—and shudder (James 2:19). Rather, faith is a trusting confidence in and reliance upon Jesus Christ as the only source of life. Those who have this faith will demonstrate it by the kindness of their actions. Relief in outward things is visible evidence of the saint's union with Christ. In his *Commentary on Corinthians*, Charles Hodge (1797–1878) wrote,

> It is not benevolence which makes a man a Christian, for then all philanthropists would be Christians. Nor is it mere piety, in the sense of reverence for God, which makes a man a Christian, for then all devout Muslims and Jews would be Christians. Morality does not make us religious, but religion makes us moral. In like manner benevolence and piety (in the wide sense) do not make men Christians, but Christianity makes them benevolent and devout.[4]

Anyone who is part of the communion of the saints will care for the needs of his brothers and sisters.

Jesus also identifies particular ways that we should respond to those in need. We should feed the hungry, stand beside the lonely, clothe the naked, and offer shelter to those who have no home. If we engage in acts of relief and kindness, it is as if we do them for Christ (Matt. 25:40). In commenting on this passage, Matthew Henry asked, "If Christ himself were among us in poverty, how readily would we relieve him? In person, how frequently would we visit him?"[5] How frequently, indeed!

Christ's final judgment, then, is similar to God's judgment upon Israel in the exile. The Father and the Son show a deep concern for the helpless. In both instances, the sheep are separated from the goats, and in both cases the failure to relieve the oppressed is the criterion of judgment. As the Scripture warns, "Faith by itself, if it is not accompanied by action, is dead" (James 2:17). The examples of Abraham and Rahab (James 2:23–25), whose works testified to their faith, illustrate this principle. Good works also reflect God's love in one's heart: "If anyone has material possessions and sees his brother in need but has no pity on him, how can the love of God be in him?" (1 John 3:17). As Christ laid down his life for us, so we should be willing to lay our lives down for one another.

A Present Reality

So far we have considered Israel's failure to fulfill God's command in the Old Testament and God's final accounting of humanity. Between these two judgments, we find that those who live in the gospel era are empowered by the work of the Holy Spirit to do good works. This was true in the early church, throughout church history, and in the church today.

From the earliest days of the church, the saints understood their obligation to be charitable, especially to other members of the Christian community (Gal. 6:10). Gospel charity was so widespread in the early church that no one was in need (Acts 4:34). Whenever there was a need, some among them contributed sufficient sums for the welfare of others. Their attitude can be summed up as follows: "What's mine is yours!" The sense of *koinonia* was palpable. Similarly Paul commanded the collection of offerings from the churches in Corinth and Galatia and even set an appointed time to receive these gifts for the needy (1 Cor. 16:1–4). He also made provision for the care of widows, warning that "if anyone does not provide for his relatives, and especially for his immediate family, he has denied the faith and is worse than an unbeliever" (1 Tim. 5:8). Like the early believers, we should notice and respond to needs within the Christian community (without ignoring unbelievers who also have needs). God's ultimate purpose is that through these generous acts, the Son will offer the Father a communion of saints that is pure, united, and undefiled.

Christian charity did not cease with the apostles. A good example comes from Eusebius, the brilliant Christian historian of the fourth century. Eusebius records that a severe pestilence and famine during his lifetime was accompanied by Emperor Maximin's persecution of the Christians. However, rather than watching the church disband,

> the heathen every where beheld a striking proof of the piety and universal benevolence of the Christians. Amidst calamities so numerous and so severe, they alone exhibited in substantial deeds, the offices of mercy and humanity. They daily employed themselves, partly in protecting and burying the bodies of the dead (for innumerable multitudes, of whom no person took care, died every day), and partly in distributing provisions to all the indigent in the whole city that were pining for hunger, whom they collected for that purpose. The consequence was, that this was extensively talked of and divulged, and all men highly extolled the God of the Christians, and confessed that they alone had approved themselves in deed and in truth the sincere worshippers of God.[6]

This was also true during Calvin's reformation of Geneva, when the church insisted that Christians had an obligation to contribute to material needs. Somewhere Calvin observed that he considered it part of his responsibility as a pastor to "raise in each member of the Christian Community the spiritual problem of his material life, of his goods, of his time, and of his capabilities, in view of freely putting them at the service of God and neighbor." Calvin practiced these principles by refusing to live a luxurious and comfortable lifestyle, especially after he became famous. When Cardinal Sadoleto visited Geneva to see where the prince of the Protestants lived, he was dumbfounded by Calvin's humble quarters.

A century later, the first churches of New England gave careful consideration to helping those in material need. In the Dutch community of Albany, New York, deacons took the lead in giving widows wheat, corn, bread, and peas. The diaconate also ran a "Butcher's Shop," the profits of which went to support the poor. The minutes from their diaconal meetings record such gifts in kind as "half a hog," "a deer," or "a quarter of a cow." Within the community there was also a "Poor House" where the homeless could stay overnight and receive food and other supplies. In Puritan Boston, Cotton Mather (1663–1728) preached occasional Sunday evening sermons for the poor. Afterwards a benevolence offering was received. Careful accounts of these transactions were kept in either the "Poor Relief Record" (First Church of Boston) or "The Sacramental Offerings" (Second Church of Boston). Some members indicated in their wills that portions of their estates were to be disbursed to the poor in the community. Mather gave generous gifts of money as well as gifts in kind to support the poor.[7]

These brief examples from church history serve to represent the many millions of Christians who have sought to maintain the communion of the saints through practical service. Although relief work often goes unrecognized, good deeds are never overlooked by God. The strength and unity of his body reflect the active care and love that the saints show to one another. Charity is a test of our commitment to the truth. Are we feeding the homeless? Do we help internationals adjust to life in the United States? Do we visit those who are in prison? Do we care for those who are suffering and dying from AIDS? If we are doing these kinds of things, then we are practicing the communion of the saints. If not, we are not loving our neighbors . . . or God.

To help maintain the communion of saints by deeds of mercy, here are three principles to follow. First, we must accept the command to give relief in outward things as a command from God designed for our spiritual growth, the encouragement of others, and the welfare of the church. Second, we must believe that as we fulfill this command, God will draw his people together in a special and intimate way. Although we cannot explain how this communion is accomplished, we will see its effects in our midst. Third, we must be joyful in our giving, so that others will praise God for what we do.

The place to begin is where we are. Is there anyone in our immediate household who has material needs? Is there anyone in our local Bible study group who would benefit from such gifts? Look around the church. Sooner or later we will hear someone talk about a need to which we can respond. We should give generously to the deacons and ask if there is any way to help them in their work. Are there any neighbors or coworkers to whom we can minister? We do not have to look far to find someone to help. Once we have someone in mind, we can ask God to give us the wisdom to know the best way to help.

By giving relief in outward things, we show our love for God and for others and thus fulfill the two greatest commandments. Then it is God's part to knit our hearts together in true spiritual communion. They will know we are Christians by our love, and the world will be changed.

TEN

Mutual Edification

Let the word of Christ dwell in you richly as you teach and admonish one another with all wisdom, and as you sing psalms, hymns and spiritual songs with gratitude in your hearts to God. (Col. 3:16)

Saints by profession are bound to maintain an holy fellowship and communion . . . in performing such . . . spiritual services as tend to their mutual edification. (Confession of Faith, 26.2)

"Good answer!" "Nice shot!" "This project is first rate!" Even a few words of encouragement can help someone become a better student, a better ballplayer, or a better worker. People love to be affirmed. What people do not always appreciate is being corrected. "Sorry, wrong answer!" "No wonder you keep missing! You have to follow through on that jump shot!" "I was hoping for better work from you this time." Such words of rebuke can be difficult to hear. Positive feedback is usually more welcome than constructive criticism.

The Confession of Faith instructs the saints to perform "such other spiritual services as tend to their mutual edification" (26.2). The spiritual services that tend to mutual edification include encouragement and correction. Words of encouragement are always a blessing, but words of correction are equally necessary. To practice the communion of the saints is to offer affirmation and admonition.

A Living Edifice

The reason the saints must correct as well as encourage one another is that we are being built together. The word *edification* has the same root as the word *edifice*, which is exactly what the saints are to become—a living edifice: "As you come to him, the living Stone—rejected by men but chosen by God and precious to him—you also, like living stones, are being built into a spiritual house to be a holy priesthood, offering spiritual sacrifices acceptable to God through Jesus Christ" (1 Peter 2:4–5).

God is building this spiritual edifice for his glory. We have not been placed in God's house by any work of our own, but by his grace. Now it is our purpose to stand for his glory. Like a master builder, God has placed us in a position where we can grow as believers and where God can also use us in the lives of others. This is the foundation upon which we should consider mutual edification.

Since mutual edification exists for the glory of God, it is not voluntary:

> We should not . . . think of fellowship with other Christians as a spiritual luxury, an optional addition to the exercises of private devotion. We should recognize rather that such fellowship is a spiritual necessity; for God has made us in such a way that our fellowship with himself is fed by our fellowship with fellow-Christians, and requires to be so fed constantly for its own deepening and enrichment.[1]

To put this another way, we are not spiritually self-sufficient. Mutual edification is a spiritual necessity. In the process of sanctification God uses other Christians like chisels to shape us more and more into the image of Christ. Thus each living stone in God's edifice is unique, vital, and essential.

The purpose of this chapter is to answer three questions about the "spiritual services" which "tend to our mutual edification." First, What spiritual services must we provide for other saints? Second, How do we provide these spiritual services in various relationships? Third, What examples from Scripture and church history help show us how to offer these services?

At Your Service

Perhaps the most obvious spiritual service that Christians offer other members of God's household is encouragement. As we have seen, God has given some gifts to others that he has not given to us. Rather than being jealous or resentful that we do not have these gifts, we should humbly recognize them in others and seek to affirm those who are using God's gifts faithfully. The gift of encouragement ultimately comes from God, who wants us to be an encouragement to one another in our spiritual work. Joseph, a Levite from Cyprus, had such an unusual aptitude for encouragement that the apostles renamed him Barnabas, which means "Son of Encouragement" (Acts 4:36). But our best model is Jesus Christ. Jesus knows all our weaknesses, shortcomings, and failures; yet he is patient and caring with us, encouraging us to do our best.

Another spiritual service we offer the other stones in God's spiritual edifice is a willingness to submit to instruction. Careful self-examination should be part of our daily or monthly devotional habit. For us to be used by God, we must be certain who we are, what we believe, and how God wants us to grow. As Christians we live under authority, first to the Scriptures and then to those who hold leadership positions in the church. The living stones in God's household must examine themselves continually to be able properly to encourage or rebuke others. As we learn the Scriptures, we begin to see ourselves as God sees us. We become willing to forgive others because we know how much we have been forgiven, and we are less prone to be critical since we know how patient and kind God has been with us. Self-examination is an important part of our spiritual service, for the good of the saints and for the glory of God.

God calls Christians to do more than encourage others and examine themselves. He also calls them to warn or rebuke those who fail to follow God's commands and live in sin. Obviously self-examination is a prerequisite for correction. That is why Jesus warned his disciples about the danger of judging others:

> Why do you look at the speck of sawdust in your brother's eye and pay no attention to the plank in your own eye? How can you say to your brother, "Let me take the speck out of your eye," when all the time there is a plank in your own eye? You hypocrite, first take the plank out of your own eye, and then you will see clearly to remove the speck from your brother's eye. (Matt. 7:3–5)

Christians who examine themselves will be able to see clearly enough to correct a brother or sister.

The Scripture commands us to "consider how we may spur one another on toward love and good deeds" (Heb. 10:24). Instead of using the words "spur on," the King James Version says that we should "provoke" one another to love and good works. The word *provoke* rightly suggests that it is appropriate to exhort and sometimes even to reprove another Christian. As it says in the Old Testament law, "Do not hate your brother in your heart. Rebuke your neighbor frankly so you will not share in his guilt" (Lev. 19:17). Such a rebuke should always be guarded by prudence and directed by love. When done properly and lovingly, this type of admonition gains far better results than the compliments of flattering lips (Prov. 28:23). A rebuke favorably received saves a person from God's wrath and judgment and restores him to the fellowship of the saints. John Calvin wrote, "We must . . . use good and brotherly correction, and thereby find the means that his faults may be buried before God, and also not come in remembrance before men."[2] Elsewhere Calvin listed the purposes of confronting those living in sin: "Discipline is like a bridle to restrain and tame those who rage against the doctrine of Christ; or like a spur to arouse those of little inclination; and also sometimes like a father's rod to chastise mildly and with the gentleness of Christ's Spirit those who have more seriously lapsed."[3]

As we apply these spiritual services, God shapes his church into the image of Christ. As living stones we are shaped into Christ's likeness, until the whole building becomes united in love and demonstrates the power of God's grace to the world. It is for God's glory that we are knit together. And if the edifice is for God's glory, then it is also for our ultimate good.

Family Matters

The primary arena for mutual edification is the family, which God has established as our primary learning community. Parents are to provide good instruction and encouragement to their children to learn Bible verses, catechism answers, and hymns or songs. Parents should testify to the special blessings they receive from the Lord throughout the day (Deut. 6:6–9, 20–25). In the same way that the Israelites spoke to their children about their deliverance from Egypt,

Christians are to speak about deliverance from sin and death through Jesus Christ. Godly parents provide a family atmosphere in which the Bible is read, prayers are heard, and praises are offered for answered prayer. Parents are to point their children in the right way with all possible help and encouragement in the fellowship of believers. The goal of this instruction is to train a child's heart to love God and live for his glory.

Effective parenting also involves admonishing children to do what is right in God's sight. Certain decisions must be made by the parent until the child is mature enough to assume personal responsibility for them. For example, parents have the responsibility to decide how much (if any) time a child may talk on the phone, watch television, or go to the mall. Parents should address matters of appropriate language, time management, and reading materials. Positive reinforcement helps encourage good decision making on the part of the child.

The father bears the primary responsibility for the spiritual tone of the family. He should direct the time of family devotions, leading in Scripture reading (with discussion and application), prayer, and singing. Devotional times need not be long, especially when there are young children in the house. But they should be regular, systematic, and joyful. The Puritans provided fathers in their congregations with manuals of suggested prayers and Scripture readings. Prayer before and after meals was used as a time of reflective devotion. Then, as now, fathers needed to lead in this area to edify their families.

How should children respond? Partly by offering encouragement and admonition to their parents. Children are not to be despised or put down but to be an example to others, including their parents (2 Tim. 3:16). Sometimes even the mouths of babes reveal the mysteries of God. At other times children observe and correct the discrepancy between what their parents say and what they do and thus help their parents become more consistent in their walk with God.

Husbands and wives should also edify one another. A proper guide is given in Ephesians 5 and 6, where Paul admonishes us "to submit to one another out of reverence for Christ" (Eph. 5:21). Paul then clarifies how this submission is carried out. The husband submits to Christ, the wife to the husband, the children to parents, and the employee to the employer (Eph. 5:22–6:9). Paul is not setting up a hierarchical system of power; rather, he is noting that whoever and wherever we are, we are to live in submission to others—no one is exempt. Husbands and wives should practice kindness, respect, honor, and love. In the context of their love covenant they are free to offer words of encouragement, advice, and counsel. In order to become instruments of mutual sanctification, husbands and wives must learn how to correct their spouses firmly and yet affectionately. They must also be able to receive words of correction without getting angry.

One minister who sought to practice these principles was the Puritan Richard Baxter (1615–91). In his reflections on his first imprisonment for preaching the gospel, Baxter commented on the courage of his wife, Margaret: "When I was carried thence to the common jail for teaching . . . I never perceived her trouble at it. She cheerfully went with me into prison; she brought her best bed thither and did much to remove the removable inconveniences of the prison. I think she had scarce ever a pleasanter time in her life than while she was with me there."[4] Margaret was Richard Baxter's most faithful friend, and he frequently consulted with her about pastoral issues that were not confidential. And he received her occasional rebukes with gratitude:

> She was very desirous that we should all have lived in a constancy of devotion and a blameless innocency. And in this respect she was the meetest helper that I could have had in the world (that ever I was acquainted with); for I was apt to be over-careless in my speech and too backward to my duty, and

she was always endeavoring to bring me to greater wariness and strictness in both. If I spoke rashly or sharply, it offended her; if I behaved (as I was apt) with too much neglect of ceremony or humble compliment to any, she would modestly tell me of it; if my very looks seemed not pleasant, she would have me amend them (which my weak pained state of body undisposed me to do); if I forgot any week to catechize my servants and familiarly instruct them personally (besides my ordinary family duties), she was troubled at my remissness.[5]

A godly wife encourages her husband to become a godly man.

Puritans like Baxter rightly believed that the family was "a little church" where God was to be worshiped and praised. As we instruct and admonish one another, God is faithful to keep his covenant promises. These blessings are for every household, and not just for families. Christian singles who live in the same home should meet regularly for Bible reading and prayer. If our homes are not holy to the Lord, then we are in danger of living like pagans. Regardless of our family associations, we are to practice giving spiritual help so that the whole household of God might be built up and encouraged.

Small Groups

Spiritual edification is mutual. The writer to the Hebrews reminds us not to "give up meeting together" (Heb. 10:24–25). Some would take this to mean attendance at a church service, but the communion of saints means much more than going to worship once a week. Because God has created us to be dependent on one another, we are to "encourage one another daily" (Heb. 3:13). When we consider the spiritual services that tend to mutual edification, we need to consider Hebrews 10 in its broadest context to include weekly worship and times of meeting in smaller groups. The Lord Jesus promised that his Spirit would be present whenever two or three are gathered in his name (Matt. 18:20). In keeping with this promise, the early Christians met throughout the week to share food and fellowship (Acts 2:41–42).

Another group to interpret Hebrews 10 broadly was the Puritans, who frequently quoted this proverb: "Have communion with few, be intimate with one. Deal justly with all, speak evil of none." Such a motto reminds us of our responsibilities as members of God's spiritual household. The New Testament gives us guidelines for encouraging one another in the household of faith. When the Puritans talked about "communion with few," they were referring to the "private meeting," "conference meeting," or "society of conference." Today these meetings would be called small groups, home Bible studies, or cell churches. The Puritans often held their meetings in private homes, where they would pray, sing hymns, discuss sermons, and generally "confer together about the things of God." These house groups were viewed as channels for the work of the Holy Spirit as "iron sharpened iron." Their meetings gave members opportunities to love, comfort, and exhort one another. They also afforded members the opportunity to demonstrate their spiritual gifts, such as teaching, which would later be integrated into the ministry of the larger church. These small groups were places where the saints received encouragement through prayer and teaching, as well as through correction and rebuke. It is in the context of a small, loving fellowship that a Christian often feels most free to share personal difficulties and discuss spiritual truths.

Small groups were also part of the Evangelical Awakening of the eighteenth century in Great Britain and America. As new converts were added to the church, they were brought into little societies for spiritual fellowship. These small groups included testimonies of conversion, confession of sin, and sharing in the joys of the Christian life.

They were not Bible studies, although each member was encouraged to study the Bible. Instead, the stress was on how to live the Christian life. Although at first ministers led these societies, increasing numbers eventually forced lay leaders to take responsibility for them.[6]

It is difficult to see how Christians can do all the one-anothering the New Testament requires without meeting in small groups for mutual edification. It is in the context of such a group that the saints experience genuine *koinonia*, that dynamic spiritual bond between Christians who have fellowship with Jesus Christ. As George Whitefield exhorted his converts:

> My brethren . . . let us plainly and freely tell one another what God has done for our souls. To this end you would do well, as others have done, to form yourselves into little companies of four or five each, and meet once a week to tell each other what is in your hearts; that you may then also pray for and comfort each other as need shall require. None but those who have experienced it can tell the unspeakable advantages of such a union and communion of souls. . . . None I think that truly loves his own soul and his brethren as himself, will be shy of opening his heart, in order to have their advice, reproof, admonition and prayers, as occasions require. A sincere person will esteem it one of the greatest blessings.[7]

Private Conference

Another type of one-anothering is meeting one on one with a bosom friend, someone with whom one can share everything, who is a partner for prayer and spiritual discussion. The Puritans referred to these meetings, in which believers would seek out a minister or a mature Christian to mentor them, as "private conferences." One example comes from *Pilgrim's Progress,* in which Faithful offers spiritual counsel to Christian so that he can press forward to the Celestial City. Contemporary Christians would probably call this discipleship. For the Puritans, such discipleship involved counseling, praying, diagnosing spiritual questions or problems, testifying to the work of the Holy Spirit, resolving doubts and fears, and giving thanks for answered prayer. Private conference provided an appropriate context for spiritual accountability, including the confession of sin.

The Bible teaches the value of mutual edification through private conference. Before Israel moved across the Jordan, Moses encouraged Joshua not to be afraid of what would happen (Deut. 1:38). He met with Joshua to remind him of God's past faithfulness in defeating two rival kings (Deut. 3:20–21). Moses exhorted Joshua not to be afraid and to believe God's promise that he would take the Israelites to the Promised Land. Honestly and lovingly, Moses encouraged and admonished Joshua to trust God. When the time came, Joshua responded obediently by commanding his officials to cross the river, and the whole fellowship entered the Promised Land. Joshua's courage and decisive leadership were the product of his mutually edifying relationship with Moses.

Another biblical example of mutual edification is the relationship between Elijah and Elisha. When God called him into the ministry, Elisha burned all his possessions, "set out to follow Elijah and became his attendant" (1 Kings 19:21). He served Elijah so faithfully that he is later referred to as the man "who used to pour water on the hands of Elijah" (2 Kings 3:11). By following a man of God, Elisha learned how to follow God for himself. Later, when Elijah was taken up into heaven, Elisha was ready to assume his mantle of leadership in ministry (2 Kings 2:13–14).

Wise Christians follow this biblical pattern. Discipleship can occur within families. When Cotton Mather gave private counsel to his daughter Katy, he took a personal interest in her struggles with salvation and fear of death. In his diary he wrote, "I thereupon made the child kneel by me; and I poured out my Cries unto the Lord, that He would lay his hands upon her, and bless her and save her, and I made her a Temple of his glory. It will be so; it will be so."[8]

Discipleship is to occur in the church as well as at home. When the Dutch settled west of Boston, the company owners were always careful to send a minister. Because of the heavy workloads, the ministers were later assisted by a lay minister called a *krankenbezoker*, or visitor of the sick. His responsibilities included leading religious services, encouraging new families who had just arrived in America, acting as a lay reader, and visiting the sick in the community.

Spiritual fellowship with one another on any level (family, small group, or one on one) involves commitment, honesty, openness, and integrity. Wherever these virtues are present, the saints enter into deep and satisfying relationships that promote their spiritual growth. In a letter to a friend, Jonathan Edwards's daughter Esther described a recent evening of mutual edification:

> O my dear how Charming it is to set and hear such excellent persons converse on the experimentals of religion. It seemed like old times. . . . I esteem *religious conversation* one of the best helps to keep up religion in the soul, excepting secret devotion, I don't know but the very best—Then what a lamentable thing that it is so neglected by God's own Children.[9]

Strengthening the Edifice

What principles are we to follow in rendering spiritual services for mutual edification? First, mutual edification depends upon ceaseless prayer. The greatest spiritual service that we can offer to others is to pray for them. Unfortunately prayer is often overlooked as a means of encouragement. It is equally effective as a means of correction. The first step in building up those who struggle with sin is to pray for them. Our prayers may lead to significant spiritual growth. Very likely the reason the Holy Spirit has brought their sin to our attention is so that we can pray for them.

As we examine ourselves before the Lord in prayer, we should seek God's Spirit for an understanding of our relationship to him. We should ask for power to live our lives in a godly and holy manner so that he can use us to encourage or admonish others. We should ask ourselves questions like these: How am I dealing with sin in my life? Am I praying for others, especially those who need admonishment? Prayer is hard work, but it is also one of the best ways to edify other believers. Dietrich Bonhoeffer has observed that "a Christian fellowship lives and exists by the intercession of its members for one another, or it collapses."[10]

Second, mutual edification involves a willingness to learn from others. It is as the Word dwells in us that we are enabled wisely to teach and to admonish through hymns and spiritual melodies (Col. 3:16). In fact, only as we properly receive encouragement and rebuke from the Scriptures are we able to grow from the encouragement and admonition that we receive from other Christians. If we cannot hear God, how can we hear each other? To practice mutual edification may involve risks to one's reputation, but this is how God works out his purposes for us and for others in his spiritual household. Are we willing to give spiritual services and to be rebuked for our actions? From time to time it is good to ask one's spouse or some other bosom friend to help us see our strengths and weaknesses.

Finally, mutual edification involves great joys and special blessings. Sometimes it may be difficult to offer encouragement or rebuke because we do not see immediate results. Sometimes we begin to understand God's working only with the passing of time. But we must not lose hope. These spiritual services are pleasing to God. Since offering them is in keeping with his command, he will be pleased when we show obedience. When we are rightly encouraged or admonished, we should offer praise to God.

George McFarland, one of the authors of this book, is a Christian schoolteacher and an elder at Tenth Presbyterian Church in Philadelphia. He remembers the special encouragement he received as he completed his doctorate in church history:

> Several years ago a couple was praying for me as I finished the final exams for my graduate work. When I received the diploma, they took my wife and me out to eat. When we finished the meal, they gave me a Hershey chocolate almond bar (my favorite) and said: "We wanted you to have this as a reminder of the evening." I certainly enjoyed that candy bar, but the sweet gesture of that act of encouragement has been far more lasting. I have kept that wrapper in my Bible as a reminder.

A few words of encouragement go a long way. Even a candy bar can become a spiritual service that tends toward mutual edification. What other spiritual services can we render for the communion of the saints?

ELEVEN

All in the Family

There is neither Jew nor Greek, slave nor free, male nor female,
for you are all one in Christ Jesus. (Gal. 3:28)

Which communion, as God offereth opportunity, is to be extended
unto all those who, in every place, call upon the name of
the Lord Jesus. (Confession of Faith, 26.2)

Ethnic diversity. Racial reconciliation. Social justice. Gender equity. Handicapped rights. It may sound like the political agenda of the radical left, but these phrases describe important themes from the Bible. The New Testament places race, class, and gender in the context of the good news about Jesus Christ.

Paul's teaching in Galatians 3:28 is a good example. The way Paul begins makes it sound as if he is writing a liberal manifesto: "There is neither Jew nor Greek, slave nor free, male nor female." If that is all he had to say about race, class, and gender he would be merely a multiculturalist, a communist, and a feminist. But his thrilling conclusion makes him biblically rather than politically correct: "for you are all one in Christ Jesus." Union with Christ overcomes racial, economic, and sexual divisions within the communion of the saints.

Jew and Greek

The Puritans who wrote the Confession of Faith did not have an obvious commitment to racial reconciliation. This is mainly because they did not live in a multicultural society. Their contact with other cultures was limited largely to what they read in books.

The record of later Reformed Christians on matters of race is mixed. The Presbyterian General Assembly condemned slavery as early as 1818. Presbyterians like Charles Hodge opposed slavery and advocated its abolition. In more recent times, the South African theologian Alan Boesak has written about what it means to be *Black and Reformed* (1984). Yet, in places like South Africa and the United States, Reformed theology has sometimes been used to justify slavery and racial oppression. Some notable Christian leaders—Jonathan Edwards (1703–58) and George Whitefield (1714–70), for example—were slaveholders. Like the rest of their countrymen, Presbyterians were divided over slavery during the Civil War. Few of them exercised strong leadership during the civil rights movement.

If the church has been soft on racism, is there something wrong with Reformed theology? Not at all. The sins of our fathers make their insight into the biblical truth about race in the communion of the saints all the more striking. The Confession of Faith states that the communion of the saints, "as God offereth opportunity, is to be extended unto *all those* who, in every place, call upon the name of the Lord Jesus." The Westminster Standards teach true biblical inclusivism. No racial or ethnic constraints are placed on the communion of saints. In Christ, we are all in the family.

The communion of the saints is thus a refreshing doctrine for these ethnically fragmented times. Racially charged events of the 1990s provided a series of reminders that racial conflict was alive and well in America: the beating of Rodney King, the confirmation hearings of Supreme Court Justice Clarence Thomas, and the murder trial of football star O. J. Simpson. During the 1992 race riots in Los Angeles, an ominous warning was spray-painted on the wall of a burned-out building: "It's not over yet." That warning has proven to be prophetic. Later the nation was buzzing over audiotapes from the boardroom at Texaco. "You know how black jelly beans agree," complained one executive. "All those black jelly beans seem to be glued to the bottom of the bag."

Racism in America is more than a black and white issue. One sequence in Spike Lee's film *Do the Right Thing* is an exposé of racial prejudice, American style. In the sequence a series of African American, Hispanic, Italian, Korean, and other actors come up to the camera and verbally abuse another ethnic group. One after another, they spew out vile racial epithets. The bigotry comes in all colors.

The New Testament speaks powerfully to the ethnic divisions of the present day. One reason for this is that it was written during racist times. In fact, the racial division between Jews and Gentiles was one of the strongest ethnic divisions in the history of the world. The letter to the Ephesians describes the difference between Jew and Greek as "the barrier, the dividing wall of hostility" (Eph. 2:14). Jews and Gentiles wore different clothes, prayed different prayers, and ate different foods. They lived in their own communities, worshiped in their own temples, and married their own kind. Intimacy between Jews and Gentiles was socially unacceptable. The two groups were so completely segregated that when Jesus asked a Samaritan woman for a drink, she said, "You are a Jew and I am a Samaritan woman. How can you ask me for a drink?" John adds an editorial comment to explain the racial climate of the day: "For Jews do not associate with Samaritans" (John 4:9; cf. Acts 10:28).

If Jews do not even associate with Gentiles, then what Paul wrote to the Galatians was a cultural bombshell: "There is neither Jew nor Greek . . . for you are all one in Christ Jesus" (Gal. 3:28). He wrote the same thing to the Ephesians: "Through the gospel the Gentiles are heirs together with Israel, members together of one body, and sharers together in the promise in Christ Jesus" (Eph. 3:6). And to the Romans: "There is no difference between Jew and Gentile—the same Lord is Lord of all" (Rom. 10:12). No difference? Why, there were all kinds of differences between Jews and Gentiles. They had practically nothing in common! Yet through union with Christ, Jewish Christians and Gentile Christians hold everything in common. We have the same Father, the same Lord, the same Spirit, the same Word, the same atonement, the same salvation, and the same sacraments. Though divided by race, we are united by grace.

The Reverend Martin Luther King Jr. once argued that "racial understanding is not something that we find but something that we must create."[1] King was right to say that racial understanding is not something we find. What we usually find is the opposite: racial misunderstanding. But as King undoubtedly would have agreed, racial understanding is not something that we are able to create on our own. Genuine racial reconciliation is something only Jesus Christ can create: "His purpose was to create in himself one new man out of the two, thus making peace, and in this one body to reconcile both of them [Jews and Gentiles] to God through the cross, by which he put to death their hostility" (Eph. 2:15b–16). Only in Christ are we reconciled to God and to one another. Only in Christ can many peoples become one people. Only in Christ can racial hostility be put to death.

What does racial reconciliation mean for the communion of saints? One thing it means is that all God's saints are supposed to worship together. God announced this intention through the prophets of the Old Testament: "All nations will gather in Jerusalem to honor the name of the LORD" (Jer. 3:17). This promise will find its ultimate fulfillment in the glorious worship of heaven:

> After this I looked and there before me was a great multitude
> that no one could count, from every nation, tribe, people and

language, standing before the throne and in front of the Lamb. They were wearing white robes and were holding palm branches in their hands. And they cried out in a loud voice:

"Salvation belongs to our God,
who sits on the throne,
and to the Lamb." (Rev. 7:9–10)

If God's ultimate purpose is for us to worship him as one, diverse, multiracial communion of saints in glory, why would we settle for anything less right now? It is sometimes said that 11:00 on a Sunday morning is the most segregated hour in America. If that is true, as it seems to be, it is a reproach to the church. How can we glorify God if we do not worship together as a reconciled community? How will the world be united to God if the church is divided (see John 17:23)?

These questions force us to draw an important conclusion about the communion of the saints: If Jews and Gentiles are one in Christ Jesus, then every Christian church is in principle a multiethnic church. The reason I say "in principle" is because some churches are not located in multiethnic communities. Since the communion of the saints does not operate on a quota system, such churches do not need to find token Christians of a different color.

However, every Christian church is in principle a multiethnic church. Imagine, for example, a village church made up entirely of members from a local African tribe. It is not a multiethnic church in reality. But because it is multiethnic in principle it will become a multiethnic church as soon as it has the opportunity. Now imagine that you are a Swede from Stockholm. If you move to that African village, will you start your own church? Of course not! The communion of the saints is to be extended to "all those who, in every place, call upon the name of the Lord Jesus." So your African brothers and sisters will welcome you into their communion. It would be unthinkable for them to do otherwise. They have always been a multiethnic church in principle. Now they will welcome the opportunity to become a multiethnic church in reality. They know that in Christ, black and white Christians are all in the family.

Slave and Free

Slaves are also members of God's family. Christians have sometimes wished that the New Testament spoke more clearly about the issue of slavery. On several occasions Paul gave instructions to slaves and their masters (see Eph. 6:5–9; Col. 3:22–25), but he did so without condemning the evils of slavery. Nor did he tell masters to free their slaves. Why not?

Part of the answer has to do with the terms and conditions of slavery in the ancient world. Slavery meant something different to Paul than it meant in, say, America during the Civil War. The other part of the answer has to do with the communion of the saints. In comparison with the unity Christians have in Jesus Christ, social and economic divisions become much less significant.

Consider Paul's argument in his epistle to Philemon, which concerns a runaway slave named Onesimus. Onesimus had run away from Philemon, but while he was on the run he met Paul and was converted to Christianity. Now Paul is sending Onesimus back to Philemon. We might expect him to instruct Philemon to release Onesimus from captivity. After all, he is now a believer in Jesus Christ. However, although Paul seems to hint that Philemon could free Onesimus, he does not say that he must. This is because Paul has a more important concern: whether or not Philemon gives Onesimus his freedom, he must welcome him as a brother in Christ: "Perhaps the reason he was separated from you for a little while was that you might have him back for good—no longer as a slave, but better than a slave, as a dear brother. He is very dear to me but even dearer to you, both as a man and as a brother in the Lord" (Philem. 15–16). The brotherhood Onesimus and Philemon now share in Christ is more important than their relationship as master and slave. Slave and free, they are both in the family because they are one in Christ.

The same unity applies to the rich and the poor in the communion of the saints. God has always had a special concern for the poor. The psalmist wrote that the "LORD secures justice for the poor and upholds the cause of the needy" (Ps. 140:12). One of the reasons God takes special care of the poor is that they are often oppressed. But God wants his people to do just the opposite, replacing oppression with compassion: "This is what the LORD Almighty says: 'Administer true justice; show mercy and compassion to one another. Do not oppress the widow or the fatherless, the alien or the poor' " (Zech. 7:9–10). What does it mean to show compassion?

> Is it not to share your food with the hungry
>> and to provide the poor wanderer with shelter—
> when you see the naked, to clothe him,
>> and not to turn away from your own flesh and blood?
>> (Isa. 58:7)

Notice the reason the Scripture gives for caring for the poor: they are "your own flesh and blood." Rich or poor, they are all in the family.

Caring for the poor is part of what it means to believe in the communion of saints. The Bible teaches that Christians have a special responsibility to care for other Christians: "Therefore, as we have opportunity, let us do good to all people, especially to those who belong to the family of believers" (Gal. 6:10). The general principle of doing good can be applied specifically to poverty within the church. Whenever we have the chance, we should care for the poor, and especially for those who belong to the communion of saints.

One good way to practice the communion of the saints is to welcome the poor as well as the rich to worship. The Book of James warns us not to show favoritism:

> Suppose a man comes into your meeting wearing a gold ring and fine clothes, and a poor man in shabby clothes also comes in. If you show special attention to the man wearing fine clothes and say, "Here's a good seat for you," but say to the poor man, "You stand there" or "Sit on the floor by my feet," have you not discriminated among yourselves and become judges with evil thoughts? (James 2:2–4)

Economic or social discrimination has no place in the church. The best and perhaps the only way to combat it is to establish warm and genuine relationships of mutual respect that cross socioeconomic boundaries. The homeless are to receive as much love and care within the communion of the saints as Wall Street executives.

Another good way to practice the communion of the saints is to eat with poor and rich alike. Jesus warned against the danger of letting class dictate your dinner plans:

> When you give a luncheon or dinner, do not invite your friends, your brothers or relatives, or your rich neighbors; if you do, they may invite you back and so you will be repaid. But when you give a banquet, invite the poor, the crippled, the lame, the blind, and you will be blessed. Although they cannot repay you, you will be repaid at the resurrection of the righteous. (Luke 14:12–15; cf. James 2:1–7)

Covered dish suppers—in which the homeless are welcomed into the church as guests or in which every church member makes a culinary contribution—can be a beautiful expression of the communion of the saints. Warm Christian hospitality, at home as well as in the church, is an excellent way to show that union with Christ overcomes class barriers.

Male and Female

Gender poses another barrier to the communion of the saints. To illustrate, consider the story of the creation of human beings, as it is sometimes retold: "The Lord God formed the man from the dust of the ground and breathed into his nostrils the breath of life, and the man became a living being. Then God said, 'I can do better than that!' And so he made woman." Does that story sound humorous or insidious? If it sounds humorous, it is probably because you like the idea that women are superior to men. If it sounds insidious, it is probably because you think that women are somewhat inferior. Either way, the story reveals something important about the human condition: Men and women are in competition with one another.

The battle of the sexes began with the fall of humanity into sin. As soon as Adam and Eve disobeyed God, they were ashamed to be seen naked, and so they made clothes for themselves (Gen. 3:7). When God asked for an explanation, Adam blamed Eve for his sin: "The woman you put here with me—she gave me some fruit from the tree, and I ate it" (Gen. 3:12). Sin brings shame and blame into human relationships. God's curse against Eve promised perpetual strife between men and women: "Your desire will be for your husband, and he will rule over you" (Gen. 3:16b). In other words, the woman will desire mastery, but the man will be her master.

The battle of the sexes rages at every level of society. It starts in elementary school, if not earlier. Boys and girls generally have different interests, different goals, and different styles of communication. Invariably they end up competing with one another. Adults do the same thing. Contemporary problems concerning abortion, marriage, divorce, welfare, and child care are all complicated by perpetual strife between men and women. The battle of the sexes even rages in the church, where the role of women is one of the most divisive issues Christians face at the start of the twenty-first century.

Jesus Christ brings an end to the battle of the sexes. Where Christ rules "there is neither male nor female, for you are all one in Christ Jesus" (Gal. 3:28). Another cultural bombshell! Union with Christ creates communion between men and women. Men and women share a common salvation and a common identity. In Christ, they are all in the family.

This does not mean that Christ eradicates the distinction between masculine and feminine. God made women different from men from the beginning. Eve was not identical to Adam but complementary. God called her "a helper suitable for him" (Gen. 2:18). It is only because men and women are not identical that they can cleave to one another and "become one flesh" (Gen. 2:24).

The Bible often distinguishes between men and women in their gifts and roles. Husbands and wives fulfill complementary functions within the family. Wives are to submit to their husbands as to the Lord. The command is comprehensive: "Now as the church submits to Christ, so also wives should submit to their husbands in everything" (Eph. 5:24). As long as her husband does not make her violate the commands of Christ, a wife must serve him.

This does not mean that Christian marriage robs women of their strength or vitality. Sarah is commended for the beauty of her obedience to Abraham (1 Peter 3:5–6), but she was hardly a wallflower. Proverbs 31 is a profile of another "wife of noble character" (Prov. 31:10). Some would call her the total woman. She is not passive but vigorous and creative. She is busy with textiles, real estate, commerce, and charity. She "watches over the affairs of her household" (Prov. 31:27). Yet she proves her submission to her husband by bringing him "good, not harm, all the days of her life" (Prov. 31:12).

The submission of a Christian wife does not give her husband license to dominate. The Lord commands the wife to submit, but he does not command her husband to make her submit. Instead, he commands the husband to love his wife to the death: "Husbands, love your wives, just as Christ loved the church and gave himself up for her" (Eph. 5:25). The wife's total submission is matched by the husband's absolute sacrifice.

Although a husband and a wife each fulfill different roles in a marriage, there is something similar about the way they fulfill them. Ephesians 5 teaches that wives and husbands are to be like Jesus Christ. Wives are to submit to their husbands as to the Lord. In other words, they are to be like Jesus Christ, who did not come down from heaven to do his will but the will of his Father in heaven (John 6:38). Husbands are to love their wives just as Christ loved the church. In other words, they are to be like Jesus Christ, who gave his life for the church (Gal. 1:4). Thus Christian wives and husbands find their unity in being like Christ to one another. Since they are "heirs together of the gracious gift of life" (1 Peter 3:7), they are both to be like Christ. When husbands and wives recognize both their equality in Christ and their complementarity in Christ they are practicing the communion of the saints.

The same dynamic is at work within the church. When it comes to salvation, men and women are equal in the sight of God. There is no difference in the way that they receive the gift of God's grace. Male and female, they are one in Christ Jesus. Furthermore, men and women share most of the same spiritual gifts and graces with one another. Nearly all the commands in the New Testament are gender-inclusive. For example, these instructions about teaching and worship are for men and women alike: "Let the word of Christ dwell in you richly as you teach and admonish one another with all wisdom, and as you sing psalms, hymns and spiritual songs with gratitude in your hearts to God" (Col. 3:16). Another example is ministries of mercy.

Women are to be as active as men in "bringing up children, showing hospitality, washing the feet of the saints, helping those in trouble and devoting [themselves] to all kinds of good deeds" (1 Tim. 5:10). The effective outreach of the church depends upon the full employment of the spiritual gifts of men and women.

The Bible still maintains a distinction between men and women for some gifts and offices in the church. The Holy Spirit "does not permit a woman to teach or to have authority over a man" (1 Tim. 2:12). God has placed spiritual oversight of the teaching of the church in the care of men ordained to the office of elder (1 Tim. 3:1–7). This restriction does not destroy the unity of men and women in Christ. Instead, it preserves harmony in God's spiritual household. The conclusion we reached earlier is worth stating again. When Christian men and women recognize both their equality in Christ and their complementarity in Christ, they are practicing the communion of the saints.

One, Big, Happy Family

Race, class, and gender are not the only things that divide the saints. The needs of the disabled are another keen biblical concern. Jesus and his disciples restored the blind, the sick, and the lame to wholeness. More importantly, the good news of salvation in Christ is for the disabled every bit as much as it is for the able-bodied. Jesus told a story about a master who sent his servant into the highways and by-ways to find guests for his great banquet: "Go out quickly into the streets and alleys of the town and bring in the poor, the crippled, the blind and the lame" (Luke 14:21).

This banquet is a picture of the communion of the saints. Everyone is invited. We all feast together because we are all one in the family of God. Jesus Christ unites wherever ethnicity, class, gender, and capability divide. In fact, our very diversity most clearly emphasizes our fundamental unity in Christ. As Manny Ortiz has written in *One New People*, "Diversity, not sameness, is the means by which God brings us to unity."[2]

The communion of the saints is always an occasion for celebration. From 1927 to 1960, Donald Grey Barnhouse served as pastor of Tenth Presbyterian Church. Dr. Barnhouse's teaching ministry extended well beyond the city limits of Philadelphia. For nearly a decade (1939–47) he taught a Bible class in New York, on the island of Manhattan. The class was one of his favorites, especially because its members were drawn from a wide variety of ethnic, denominational, and social backgrounds. Barnhouse saw the class as a microcosm of the communion of the saints, and he loved to begin class with these joyful words: "Here we have all classes of people—rich, poor, well-educated, illiterate. . . . Here are brothers and sisters in Christ!"[3]

TWELVE

Worldwide Communion

*People will come from east and west and north and south, and will
take their places at the feast in the kingdom of God. (Luke 13:29)*

*Which communion, as God offereth opportunity, is to be extended
unto all those who, in every place, call upon the name of
the Lord Jesus. (Confession of Faith, 26.2)*

The Reverend Howard Blair, one of the authors of this book, served
as a missionary to Japan for more than four decades, during which he
learned to appreciate the words of a hymn by John Oxenham:

> In Christ there is no East or West
>   In Him no South or North;
> But one great fellowship of love
>   Throughout the whole wide earth.

Blair remembers the exact moment when Oxenham's words passed
from poetry into experience. He writes:

> My wife and I were newly arrived in Japan to begin our mis-
> sionary careers. Only a few years had passed since the end of

World War II. On our first Sunday there we attended a church that was meeting in a public hall since no church building was available. We stood and sang together in Japanese the hymn, "What a Friend We Have in Jesus." As I sang along in English, I was soon overwhelmed with feelings of joy and love for these Japanese men and women singing so heartily around me. People who very recently had been our enemies in war were my brothers and sisters in Christ. We shared the same precious faith, the same love for our Savior. Tears filled my eyes that day as the reality of the worldwide communion of saints gripped me, perhaps for the first time.

One of the privileges of serving as a missionary in a foreign culture is the vivid awareness one gains of the worldwide communion of saints. A Christian can go anywhere in the world and immediately experience the love and embrace of brothers and sisters whom he or she has never met. Stronger than the bonds of blood relationships are the ties that bind one Christian to another, even when they cannot speak the same language.

The Cosmic Plan

Many Christians are familiar with the hymn by John Newton (1725–1807) that begins "Glorious things of thee are spoken, Zion, city of our God." Fewer Christians know that Newton's text comes from Psalm 87, which celebrates the diverse unity of the city of God:

> Glorious things are said of you,
>   O city of God:
> "I will record Rahab [Egypt] and Babylon
>   among those who acknowledge me—

Philistia too, and Tyre, along with Cush [Ethiopia]—
   and will say, 'This one was born in Zion.' " (Ps. 87:3–4)

Marvelous prophecy! What is so glorious about the city of God is that people from many nations will be numbered among its citizens.

From the beginning it has been God's plan to fill his eternal kingdom with men, women, and children from all languages and cultures. The glorious vision of the worldwide communion of saints surfaces again and again in the Old Testament. To Abraham the promise is given: "All peoples on earth will be blessed through you" (Gen. 12:3). The Son of God received the same promise: "I will make the nations your inheritance" (Ps. 2:8). The prophetic word came through Isaiah to the Messiah, Jesus Christ:

"It is too small a thing for you to be my servant
   to restore the tribes of Jacob
   and bring back those of Israel I have kept.
I will also make you a light for the Gentiles,
   that you may bring my salvation to the ends of the earth."
      (Isa. 49:6)

Anything less than the worldwide communion of the saints apparently would be beneath God's dignity.

The vision becomes clearer in the New Testament. Jesus Christ came to his own people, "but his own did not receive him" (John 1:11). The meaning of this rejection is made clear in Jesus' parable about a lord who invited honored guests to a great banquet (Luke 14:16–24). When they refused to attend, he commanded his servants: "Go out quickly into the streets and alleys of the town and bring in the poor, the crippled, the blind and the lame" (Luke 14:21). Yet there was still room at the table, so the host ordered his servants to go out into the roads and country lanes to make people come in and fill his house. Similarly Jesus promised that "people will come from east and west and north and south, and will take their places at the feast in the kingdom of God" (Luke 13:29).

A full house was God's eternal plan. After Jesus rose from the dead, he met with his disciples and "opened their minds so they could understand the Scriptures" (Luke 24:45). He told them, "This is what is written: The Christ will suffer and rise from the dead on the third day, and repentance and forgiveness of sins will be preached in his name to all nations" (Luke 24:46–47). This was God's plan from all eternity: first Calvary, then Easter, then the gospel for all nations. After the resurrection, the plan became a command: "Go and make disciples of all nations" (Matt. 28:19). Then the command became a promise: "You will be my witnesses in Jerusalem, and in all Judea and Samaria, and to the ends of the earth" (Acts 1:8).

The promise became a reality for the apostle John, who was given a vision of the universal church. John wrote:

> After this I looked and there before me was a great multitude that no one could count, from every nation, tribe, people and language, standing before the throne, and in front of the Lamb. They were wearing white robes and were holding palm branches in their hands. And they cried out in a loud voice:
>
> "Salvation belongs to our God,
> who sits on the throne,
> and to the Lamb." (Rev. 7:9–10)

This is the culmination, the end toward which God is moving all human history—the worldwide community of saints worshiping before his heavenly throne. God's glory, grace, and holiness will be reflected in the diverse peoples he has called from every nation and culture. "God's intentions aren't just personal; they are corporate as well.

From the beginning our God has longed to create for Himself a community that would reign with Him forever. He plans (and He has already begun) to bring into being a new international community of reconciliation, peace, and celebration. . . . We will be one in Christ, worshiping our God as one gigantic family."[1]

Into All the World

The history of the church is the story of the progress of the communion of saints. Beginning from Jerusalem, the good news of salvation spread out through Judea, up into Samaria, and on into the cities of the Gentiles. By the time the apostle Paul addressed his letter to the church at Rome in A.D. 57 or 58, he could write, "From Jerusalem all the way around to Illyricum [Albania] I have fully proclaimed the gospel of Christ" (Rom. 15:19).

One hundred years later there were flourishing churches in nearly all the provinces between Syria and Rome—in Alexandria and Carthage and up into Gaul. By A.D. 250 a significant Christian minority existed in almost every province of the Roman Empire and beyond. During the third century the gospel began more thoroughly to penetrate the countryside around the urban centers. Fifty years later Christians formed a majority of the population in parts of North Africa and Asia Minor. Church historian Kenneth Scott Latourette concludes: "Never in so short a time has any other religious faith, or, for, that matter, any other set of ideas, religious, political, or economic, without the aid of physical force, or of social or cultural prestige, achieved so commanding a position in such an important culture."[2]

In succeeding centuries missionaries carried the gospel to the barbarian tribes of Europe. In the fifth century Patrick evangelized Ireland. The Irish monasticism of the sixth century arose on the foundations of Patrick's biblical and evangelical preaching. The monasteries in turn became centers for learning and missions. Irish monks were zealous missionaries throughout Britain and on the Continent. English missionaries then planted the gospel in Holland, Denmark, and Germany. Notable among these was Wynfrith (687–754), better known as Boniface, the apostle to the Germans. Like a living flame, the gospel spread from nation to nation and people to people.

The boundaries of Christendom greatly increased during the ninth, tenth, and eleventh centuries. This expansion came despite the loss of North Africa and the Near East to the Muslims, the decline of the papacy, and the turmoil of political disintegration. Bohemia, Moravia, Poland, Norway, Iceland, Greenland, Sweden, Hungary, Bulgaria, and Russia were all brought into the fold. Some came through the work of missionaries, more through the conversion of kings and princes who, at least nominally, brought their followers with them to Christ.

The next period of church expansion came with the widespread missionary activity of the Jesuits in the sixteenth and seventeenth centuries, in the newly discovered Western hemisphere and in the Far East. The most famous of the Jesuit missionaries was Francis Xavier (1506–1622), who evangelized in India and Japan with remarkable success. Francis was trying to enter China when he died at the age of forty-six. The Franciscans and the Dominicans also engaged in missionary activity in South America, Vietnam, and the Philippine Islands. Tens of thousands of courageous and dedicated priests contributed to the almost complete Christianization of these areas. Superficial though it may have been, some of this evangelistic work laid the foundation for the remarkable growth of the evangelical churches in the Philippines and Latin America today.

The age of Protestant missions began in the eighteenth century.

The Moravians led the way, sending out hundreds of missionaries from England and Germany. William Carey (1761–1834), often known as the father of modern missions, began his work in India in 1796. Soon Protestant missions spread to all parts of the world through church and independent mission societies.

The nineteenth century also saw the first penetration of the vast inland areas of China and Africa with the gospel. These were the days of outstanding missionary pioneers like Hudson Taylor (1832–1905) in China, Robert Moffat (1795–1883) and David Livingstone (1813–73) in Africa, Adoniram Judson (1788–1850) in Burma, James Hepburn (1815–1911) in Japan, and many others. England was the world's great superpower of the nineteenth century, and England sent the largest number of missionaries to the world. At the same time, missionaries within America sought to reach African slaves and Native American Indians with the gospel.

A World Christian Community

By 1942 the Anglican Archbishop William Temple could speak of a "Christian fellowship which now extends into almost every nation" as "the great new fact of our era." In the providence of God, the extension of Western domination into Africa, Asia, and the Americas served as a vehicle for the propagation of the gospel throughout the world. The decades following World War II were to see a general retreat of the West as one country after another shook off the colonial yoke. Nevertheless the churches in most of those lands continued to show healthy growth and in time to send their own missionaries throughout the world.

Today it is estimated that around the world an average of between sixty-five thousand and seventy thousand people become believers in Christ every day. In Africa south of the Sahara Desert and in Latin

America—particularly Brazil, Chile, and the Central American republics—the dramatic growth of the evangelical Christian community continues unabated. Statistics indicate that there were perhaps fifty thousand evangelical Christians in Latin America on the eve of World War II; today they number some forty million. In Asia, two countries long closed to the gospel—Nepal and Mongolia—now have a growing Christian presence. But perhaps the most remarkable story comes from China. Foreign missionaries were driven out of China in 1949, and the church there underwent a most severe persecution. The result? Today there are tens of millions more followers of Christ than there were in 1949.

What this all adds up to is that God, for his glory, is building a worldwide community of saints. The Spirit of God is at work—even in the strongholds of Buddhism, Hinduism, and Islam—to join men, women, and children in union with Christ and therefore in communion with one another. The diversity of cultures, languages, and people groups in the communion of the saints is God's idea. He is bringing greater glory to himself out of our diversity. To believe in the communion of saints is to

> recognize and celebrate the admirable power of our God, which unites believers of every nation, age, condition and sex, often separated from one another by such vast intervening space of land and sea, of such dissimilar capacities and tempers, and engaged in such diversified pursuits; and so closely conjoins them by one Spirit, that they most harmoniously concur in the same sentiments and feelings respecting God and Christ, and in the same devout prayers and praises, and discern in each other, with mutual congratulation and applause, the same effects of the same divine grace; so that, even at their first meeting, a most delightful interchange of love often arises.[3]

Embracing the Universal Church

In addition to recognizing and celebrating our oneness in Christ, what else can we do to experience the reality of the worldwide communion of saints? To begin with, we can increase our knowledge of the universal church. A Christian who believes in the communion of saints is eager for news about the church in other lands. Reading articles and books is one way to enter into fellowship with the circumstances of brothers and sisters in other lands. Learning about their condition helps us sympathize with those who experience oppression.

Sympathy for fellow Christians drives us to our knees to pray for them. Most international news stories suggest urgent themes for our intercession. Where there is war, pray for peace; where there is division, pray for unity; where there is persecution, pray for deliverance; where there is famine, pray for bread.

The apostle Paul teaches us how to intercede for the worldwide community of the saints. Again and again he earnestly prays for believers in the churches scattered around the Roman world. He prays not only for Christians he knew personally but also for churches with whom he had no direct contact. Prayer is the refrain of Paul's epistles:

God . . . is my witness how constantly I remember you in my prayers at all times (Rom. 1:9).

I have not stopped giving thanks for you, remembering you in my prayers (Eph. 1:16).

In all my prayers for all of you, I always pray with joy (Phil. 1:4).

We have not stopped praying for you (Col. 1:9).

We always thank God for you, mentioning you in our prayers (1 Thess. 1:2).

We constantly pray for you (2 Thess. 1:11).

How does Paul pray for these congregations? He prays that they would increase and abound in love, that they would be filled with knowledge and spiritual understanding, and that they would be strengthened for perseverance and holiness. He also prays that Jesus Christ would be glorified in them. Paul's frequent references to his prayer life are of more than autobiographical interest. We are to follow his example as he follows the example of Christ (1 Cor. 11:1). Among other things, that means praying for the saints around the world.

God loves to answer the prayers that the saints offer for one another. It is in response to our prayers that God has chosen to do his work in this world. At the same time, we will find that praying kingdom prayers enriches our fellowship with the saints. To pray for God's will to be done, his kingdom to come, and his name to be glorified in the worldwide church is to participate in the communion of saints.

We need to pray especially for our fellow Christians who are suffering oppression. Reports indicate that persecution of Christians reached an all-time high in the twentieth century. In her book on the persecuted church, Nina Shea wrote:

> Millions of American Christians pray in their churches each week, oblivious to the fact that Christians in many parts of the world suffer brutal torture, arrest, imprisonment and even death—their homes and communities laid waste—for no other reason than that they are Christians. The shocking, untold story of our time is that more Christians have died this century simply for being Christians than in the first nineteen

centuries after the birth of Christ. They have been persecuted and martyred before an unknowing, indifferent world and a largely silent Christian community.[4]

In 1996 alone, more than one hundred thousand Christians were martyred for their faith.[5] It is further estimated that nearly two hundred million of those who live in a state of chronic hunger are believers in Jesus Christ.[6]

As this is being written, word has just come of another martyr for Christ in China:

> On September 4, a subtraining center led by graduates of our SCI (Sharing Christ Internationally) ministry was raided by the local police. Thirty young people in training were arrested. All were beaten severely. The police told them, "If you agree not to preach the gospel and to attend such illegal meetings, you will be set free." None of the young believers was willing to compromise his faith. The police singled out Liu Hai Tao for further punishment in an effort to raise fear among the others. He was beaten several times a day. On October 17 he died, like Stephen, for the Lord. When he died, his hands and feet were in chains. He was nineteen years old. After his death many young pastors and evangelists heard his story. They sent thousands of letters to his parents in Henan province. They told them they will follow Liu's example and will continue the unfinished task.

The brave Chinese evangelists mentioned in the electronic message believe in the communion of saints, for they have experienced what Paul meant when he wrote, "If one part suffers, every part suffers with it" (1 Cor. 12:26). If we also believe in the communion of the saints, then some of the missionary letters and prayer updates that we receive should be sprinkled generously with our tears. Earnest prayer for fellow believers fulfills the injunction of Hebrews 13:3: "Remember those in prison as if you were their fellow prisoners, and those who are mistreated as if you yourselves were suffering."

As we are able, we must alleviate suffering and want among our brothers and sisters, including those whom we have never met. Christians as well as non-Christians suffer the effects of poverty, famine, and inadequate medical facilities. Here again, the apostle Paul set an example for us in meeting the material needs of the saints. Paul considered charity to be essential to Christian faith. His third missionary journey was partly a fundraiser for Jewish Christians living in poverty. He constantly reminded Gentile Christians to take up offerings for their needy brothers and sisters in Jerusalem. He mentions this effort in both of his letters to the Corinthians, devoting as much as two whole chapters to the subject (2 Cor. 8–9). Paul considered the conveyance of the offering to Jerusalem so important that he insisted on going there himself, even at the risk of his life (Acts 21:13). Christian relief and development organizations give us ample opportunity to follow Paul's example of mercy for the saints.

Another way to experience the reality of the worldwide communion of the saints is to seek opportunities for face-to-face fellowship with Christians who differ from us in race, national origin, culture, or custom—even if we have to venture outside our comfort zones. Spending time with international visitors is an especially good spiritual investment. Many Christian internationals return to their homelands with a zeal for sharing the gospel. They are likely to be more effective than foreign missionaries in evangelism because they already understand their own language and culture. The more teaching, fellowship, and support they receive from Western Christians, the more effective they will be in gospel outreach. International Christians also have something to offer their hosts. Their appreciation for Western Christianity teaches us what to treasure in our churches. At the same time, their insight into the sins of Western culture shows us new areas for Christian obedience.

A belief in the communion of saints inevitably will lead to an increased concern for those who are not yet united to Christ. All believers in Jesus Christ—whoever and wherever they are—are related to us as family members. When we recognize the beauty of this worldwide family, we will want to become actively involved in the task of world missions. To put this another way, we will want those who have never heard the gospel to become part of the family and thus fulfill God's ancient promise: "Those who were not told about him will see, and those who have not heard will understand" (Rom. 15:21; cf. Isa. 52:15).

We can support the worldwide work of the gospel through prayer and financial support, and perhaps even with our careers, if God so leads. We will do this so that God's lost children may be found and brought into the rich fellowship of the communion of the saints. This was the reason for the apostle John's eagerness to proclaim the gospel: "so that you also may have fellowship with us. And our fellowship is with the Father and with his Son, Jesus Christ" (1 John 1:3).

Up to this point we have been thinking of what we as individuals can do to enhance our awareness of the worldwide communion of saints—and we can do much, as we have seen. But we can do even more as we work together with our fellow Christians in our local churches. Churches that send out their members as career missionaries and then pray knowledgeably for their ministries will have a more lively sense of the worldwide communion of the saints.

Beyond that, many churches have organized short-term mission trips abroad for a group of their members. For ten days to two weeks participants build churches, teach English classes, assist in evangelism, or give aid in the areas of health and medicine. These trips enable members of the sending congregations to contribute tangibly to the ministries of Christians and their churches in a different culture. Working and worshiping side by side with Christians from other lands, many American Christians have formed lasting friendships as they continue to participate in a particular ministry through prayer and giving financial aid. It is easy to sing of "one great fellowship of love/Throughout the whole wide earth," but it is in working and worshiping together that strong bonds of love are forged—even when we speak different languages.

Something else American churches can do, and are doing, is to link with churches in other cultures in a sister-church relationship. This is now being done on a significant scale with the growing churches of the former Soviet Union. The relationship is reciprocal. American churches can offer much encouragement through their prayers and material aid. At the same time, the sister church—often struggling in difficult circumstances—brings spiritual challenge and encouragement to the American church. This comes about as members from each church pray for and, on occasion, visit one another.

Christian fellowship flows in every direction. As we open our hearts to the community of believers around the world, we receive far more than we give. The apostle Paul had much to offer the Christians in Rome. He wrote them what is perhaps the greatest theological treatise in the history of the church. Yet even Paul knew that the Roman Christians, whom he had never met, also had something to offer him. He wrote: "I long to see you so that I may impart to you some spiritual gift to make you strong—that is, that you and I may be mutually encouraged by each other's faith" (Rom. 1:11–12). Like Paul, we gain strength, encouragement, and spiritual insight from fellowship with the worldwide communion of saints. John Oxenham's hymn concludes:

> In Christ now meet both East and West,
>   In Him meet South and North;
> All Christly souls are one in Him
>   Throughout the whole wide earth.

THIRTEEN

For All the Saints

But our citizenship is in heaven. And we eagerly await a Savior from there, the Lord Jesus Christ, who, by the power that enables him to bring everything under his control, will transform our lowly bodies so that they will be like his glorious body. (Phil. 3:20–21)

All saints, that are united to Jesus Christ their Head, by His Spirit, and by faith, have fellowship with Him in His . . . glory. (Confession of Faith, 26.1)

William Walsham How (1823–97) has written a beautiful hymn about the entrance of the saints into glory. The hymn is entitled "For All the Saints," and its closing stanzas are especially moving:

> But lo! there breaks a yet more glorious day;
> the saints triumphant rise in bright array;
> the King of glory passes on his way.
> Alleluia! Alleluia!
>
> From earth's wide bounds, from ocean's farthest coast,
> through gates of pearl streams in the countless host,

singing to Father, Son, and Holy Ghost.
Alleluia! Alleluia!

How's hymn depicts the saints streaming into God's eternal kingdom like a conquering army. Row upon row, rank upon rank, as far as the eye can see, the saints are marching into glory. It is a thrilling picture of the glorious communion of the saints.

Seeing Is Becoming

In order for the saints to enter into heavenly communion they must first be glorified. In the simplest of terms, the apostle John explained how this glorification occurs: "Dear friends, now we are children of God, and what we will be has not yet been made known. But we know that when he [Christ] appears, we shall be like him, for we shall see him as he is" (1 John 3:2). This verse teaches when the saints will be glorified: at the appearance or second coming of Jesus Christ. As the apostle Paul also taught, "When Christ, who is your life, appears, then you also will appear with him in glory" (Col. 3:4). This glorious transformation will take place at the same time as the resurrection of the body. Resurrection and glorification will be simultaneous, for the saints will be "raised in glory" (1 Cor. 15:43).

John also teaches how the saints will be glorified: by seeing Jesus Christ as he is. Seeing Christ in this way is sometimes called the beatific vision. It is part of what Paul had in mind when he testified that God "made his light shine in our hearts to give us the light of the knowledge of the glory of God in the face of Christ" (2 Cor. 4:6). The glory of God is revealed in the face of Jesus Christ. The saints catch a glimpse of that glory already in the present life, but it is no more than a glimpse: "Now we see but a poor reflection as in a mirror. But [when Christ returns,] then we shall see face to face" (1 Cor. 13:12a).

Despite his many sufferings, Job never lost his hope that he would meet his Savior face to face at the resurrection. The idea of seeing God with his own eyes filled him with such great joy that he could hardly contain himself:

> I know that my Redeemer lives,
>   and that in the end he will stand upon the earth.
> And after my skin has been destroyed,
>   yet in my flesh I will see God;
> I myself will see him
>   with my own eyes—I, and not another.
>   How my heart yearns within me! (Job 19:25–27)

The last chapter in the Bible makes the same promise: "The throne of God and of the Lamb will be in the [heavenly] city, and his servants will serve him. They will see his face" (Rev. 22:3). When Jesus told his disciples, "Blessed are the pure in heart, for they will see God" (Matt. 5:8), he was not using simply a figure of speech. The pure in heart will see God, face to face, when they gaze upon the Lord Jesus Christ in all his glory.

The prospect of seeing the glory of Christ captured the imagination of the Puritans. Many Puritan gravestones in America depict a human face with eyes open wide, ready to gaze on the face of Jesus Christ. In one of his *Meditations*, the New England poet Edward Taylor expressed the same hope in a poetic couplet:

> Oh! Glorious Body! Pull my eye lids ope:
>   Make my quick Eye, Lord, thy brisk Glory greet.

The Oxford theologian John Owen spoke of the *"Beholding of the Glory of Christ"* as *"one of the greatest Privileges and Advancements that Believers are capable of."*[1] The Scottish divine Thomas Boston described the beatific vision in these words:

They [the saints] shall see Jesus Christ, God and man, with their bodily eyes, as He will never lay aside the human nature. They will behold that glorious blessed body, which is personally united to the divine nature, and exalted above principalities and powers and every name that is named. There we shall see, with our eyes, that very body which was born of Mary at Bethlehem, and crucified at Jerusalem between two thieves: the blessed head that was crowned with thorns; the face that was spit upon; the hands and feet that were nailed to the cross; all shining with inconceivable glory. The glory of the man Christ will attract the eyes of all the saints.[2]

What happens when someone sees God? We are given a hint in the account of one saint who caught a glimpse of God in the Old Testament. When Moses met with God on Mount Horeb, he asked to see God's glory. He was not allowed to see God's glorious face because no one could see God and live. However, while he was covered with God's hand in a cleft in the rock, Moses was allowed to peek at the back of God's glory as it passed by. Yet even the back of the glory of God was marvelously glorious! "When Moses came down from Mount Sinai with the two tablets of the Testimony in his hands, he was not aware that his face was radiant because he had spoken with the LORD. When Aaron and all the Israelites saw Moses, his face was radiant, and they were afraid to come near him" (Exod. 34:29–30). Once Moses had gazed upon God, his face became unbearably glorious. It reflected and radiated the glory of God. To see God is to be transformed into his glorious likeness.

The same thing will happen when we see Jesus Christ for ourselves. Seeing the Savior will glorify the saints. When Christ appears, "we shall be like him, for we shall see him as he is" (1 John 3:2). In other words, to see Christ as he is means becoming what he is. Since Christ is glorious in his resurrection body, we will become glorious in our resurrection bodies. God predestined us "to be conformed to the likeness of his Son" (Rom. 8:29). "And just as we have borne the likeness of the earthly man, so shall we bear the likeness of the man from heaven" (1 Cor. 15:49).

Glorification will involve a physical transformation: "By the power that enables him to bring everything under his control, the Lord Jesus Christ will transform our lowly bodies so that they will be like his glorious body" (Phil. 3:21). Yet this glorious resurrection body will receive its life from the Holy Spirit (Rom. 8:11), which is why the Scriptures also call it "a spiritual body" (1 Cor. 15:44). When the saints see the glorious visage of Jesus Christ they will be transformed, body and soul, into the glorious image of God.

The Westminster Larger Catechism summarizes the biblical teaching about glorification as follows: "The bodies of the just, by the Spirit of Christ, and by virtue of his resurrection as their head, shall be raised in power, spiritual, and incorruptible, and made like to his glorious body" (A. 87). Glorification is the complete, permanent, and instantaneous transformation of the body and soul of the resurrected believer into the glorious image of the risen Christ.

All Together Then

Glorification differs from other events in the history of salvation in two respects. First, it lies in the future. The saints have yet to become fully united to Christ in his glory. Glorification is the one aspect of union with Christ that we have yet to experience. Second, glorification will happen to all the saints all at once. Communion with Christ in glory will be for all the saints. Glorification will be the consummation of the communion of the saints.

Christians take most of the steps of salvation at their own pace. This is obviously the case with regeneration. The Holy Spirit enters various minds and hearts at different times to draw them to faith in Christ. As Jesus told Nicodemus, "The wind blows wherever it pleases. You hear its sound, but you cannot tell where it comes from or where it is going. So it is with everyone born of the Spirit" (John 3:8). The same is true with justification. Since justification is by faith, a sinner is justified whenever he or she first trusts in Christ for salvation, which happens at a different time and place for every believer. Christians are also sanctified at their own pace. We do not all become like Christ in exactly the same way at exactly the same time. Regeneration, justification, and sanctification happen to various saints at various times.

By contrast, glorification will happen to all the saints at the same time. We will all be glorified all of a sudden. The Scripture says that the glorious transformation of the saints will happen "in a flash, in the twinkling of an eye, at the last trumpet. For the trumpet will sound, the dead will be raised imperishable, and we will be changed" (1 Cor. 15:52). All the saints, living and dead, will be changed into glory together. There will be a simultaneous, instantaneous glorification of the whole communion of the saints in Christ. To quote again from the Larger Catechism, the saints will be

> made perfectly holy and happy both in body and soul, in the company of innumerable saints and angels, but especially in the immediate vision and fruition of God the Father, of our Lord Jesus Christ, and of the Holy Spirit, to all eternity. And this is the perfect and full communion, which the members of the invisible church shall enjoy with Christ in glory, at the resurrection and day of judgment. (A. 90)

Since all the saints will be glorified at the same time, it is not surprising that the New Testament generally speaks of glorification in the plural. Christ will return in order "to be glorified in his holy people" (2 Thess. 1:10). His glory "will be revealed in us" (Rom. 8:18). To

God "be glory in the church" (Eph. 3:21). Christ "will transform our lowly bodies so that they will be like his glorious body" (Phil. 3:21). In every case, glorification belongs to the whole communion of saints. The Bible teaches us to speak of *our* glorification rather than *my* glorification.

The fact that glorification is for all the saints explains why the New Testament speaks of sharing in God's glory. For example, Paul told the Romans, "We share in his sufferings in order that we may also share in his glory" (Rom. 8:17). Believers have been called to "share in the glory of our Lord Jesus Christ" (2 Thess. 2:14), and they hope to "share in the glory to be revealed" (1 Peter 5:1). As Christ shares his glory with us, we share in his glory with him and with one another. Part of what makes glorification so glorious is that it is a shared experience. Sinclair Ferguson writes:

> What a tremendously exciting prospect this is! Here we are, at such different stages of Christian experience: some who have been Christians for many years, others converted recently; some highly gifted, others weak in both grace and gifts. Moreover, how many thousands and millions of God's children have passed out of this world before us? But on that day we shall all together share in the glorification of Jesus, and our glorification with him. It is as though God has said to himself: 'I have given my children so much as individuals and as little groups; but now, in this last decisive act, in the public proclamation and appearance of my Son—I will give all of them my final special blessing all at once!'[3]

Overcoming All the Obstacles

Once all the saints have been glorified together, we will enter into intimate, eternal, and unbroken communion with one another. To be in heaven is to be forever united to Christ and to all who love him. One of the first theologians to emphasize the communion of the saints in glory was Augustine, who taught that the loving communion of the saints in heaven will flow from the communion that exists within the Trinity. The holy society that God the Father, God the Son, and God the Holy Spirit already enjoy will widen to include all the saints.

The Puritans also looked forward to the communion of the saints in glory, which they liked to call the "society of heaven." By "society" they meant a community of close relationships. Thomas Boston believed that the "chief part of heaven's happiness lies in the blessed society which the saints shall have" with other saints and with the Lord.[4] Jonathan Edwards preferred to speak of the glorious communion of the saints as a "family." In one of his *Miscellanies*, Edwards wrote that heaven is a "world of love" because there is an "eternal society or family in the Godhead in the Trinity of persons." In other words, the Holy Trinity itself is a sort of family. That family will be expanded in glory when God will share his "infinitely dear and incomprehensible mutual love" with the saints and admit them "into the divine family as his son's wife."

It sounds like a perfect family (and it is!), especially since God's family on earth often seems rather dysfunctional. This book began by mentioning some of the divisions that hinder the communion of the saints. At present, the saints are divided by time, geography, ethnicity, class, gender, and schism. It is not until they commune in glory that these obstacles will be overcome. But overcome they will be!

Communion in glory will unite the saints across time. Christians often look forward to meeting the heroes and heroines of the faith when they get to heaven. They imagine what it will be like to shake hands with Samson, to go fishing with Peter, or to raise a glass of ale with Martin Luther. They also long to be reunited with family members and friends who have gone to be with the Lord. These are not idle notions. The communion of saints is one of the promised blessings of heaven.

The transfiguration of Jesus Christ shows how glory can rule over history to establish the eternal communion of the saints. When Jesus was transfigured on the mountainside, "his face shone like the sun, and his clothes became as white as the light" (Matt. 17:2). But Jesus was not alone in his glory, for "just then there appeared before them Moses and Elijah, talking with Jesus" (Matt. 17:3). Although they lived centuries apart, Moses and Elijah enjoyed intimate communion with Christ and with one another.

Another glimpse of the glorious communion of saints across time comes near the end of the Book of Hebrews, in the catalogue of the heroes and heroines of the Old Testament: "These were all commended for their faith, yet none of them received what had been promised" (Heb. 11:39). Why not? Why didn't they receive what God promised them? Because "God had planned something better for us so that only together with us would they be made perfect" (Heb. 11:40). As much as we look forward to meeting the saints of the Old Testament, they look forward to meeting us even more! Their redemption will not be complete until they are perfected together with us. They will not be glorified until we are glorified, for the communion of the saints in glory will include all God's people throughout all of history.

The communion of the saints in glory will also overcome the obstacles raised by geography. Now the saints are scattered throughout the whole wide world. Even the most well-traveled Christians have met just a handful of all the believers there are to meet. It would take more than a thousand lifetimes to visit all the churches in the world. But when Christ appears he will gather all the saints into one place. They will no longer be separated by space, but they will live in one city—the heavenly Jerusalem (Rev. 21), where all the saints will live in the same zip code.

For many years the Oxford don C. S. Lewis (1898–1963) corresponded in Latin with a priest from Verona named Don Giovanni Calabria. Because they were separated by the English Channel and the Italian Alps, the two men never met in person. Yet Lewis longed for the day when glory would overcome geography and they would meet face to face. He wrote: "Now indeed mountains and seas divide us; nor do I know what your appearance is in the body. God grant, on that day hereafter, day of the resurrection of the body, yes, and of all things made, beyond our telling, new—God grant us, on that Day, to meet."[5]

The communion of the saints in glory will overcome the barriers of ethnicity, class, and gender. The glorified saints will make up "a great multitude that no one could count, from every nation, tribe, people and language" (Rev. 7:9). This verse mentions different forms of political, ethnic, and cultural distinction. It teaches that every people group will be represented in God's heavenly community. All the saints will form one communion to praise one God with one voice at one time. They will all sit down at the wedding supper of the Lamb together (Rev. 19:9).

Even the strife between men and women will be overcome in heaven. Jesus taught that "at the resurrection people will neither marry nor be given in marriage; they will be like the angels in heaven" (Matt. 22:30). This text suggests that gender relationships will be so transformed that men and women will live together in perfect love and harmony. They will be like the angels, or perhaps like affectionate siblings to one another.

Finally, the communion of the saints in glory will overcome all the schisms within the Christian church. Shortly before he died, Jesus offered this prayer for all the saints:

> I pray also for those who will believe in me through their message, that all of them may be one, Father, just as you are in me and I am in you. May they also be in us so that the world may believe that you have sent me. I have given them the glory

that you gave me, that they may be one as we are one: I in them and you in me. May they be brought to complete unity to let the world know that you sent me and have loved them even as you have loved me. (John 17:20–23)

This prayer sometimes seems to have gone unanswered. The church is divided in its doctrine, practice, and worship. Sometimes it is hard to get Christians to agree on much of anything.

However, when the saints commune in glory, Jesus' prayer for the unity of the church will be fully answered. There all disputes will come to an end. Paul will embrace Barnabas (see Acts 15:37–39), and Euodia and Syntyche will agree with each other in the Lord (see Phil. 4:2). There all denominational boundaries will be erased; Presbyterians and Baptists will worship arm in arm. There all the saints will have perfect communion with one another because they will all be one in Christ Jesus. Like many Christians, Richard Baxter longed to take his place in that "Family of Heaven . . . where there is no division, nor dissimilitude, nor differing judgments, nor disaffection, nor strangeness, but all are one in Christ, who is one with the Father."[6]

Communion with Christ in Glory

As wonderful as it is to contemplate the communion of the saints in glory, heaven is more than just a great place to socialize. The best thing about heaven is that God is there, in all the fullness of his triune being. Our brightest hope is not communion with the saints, as wonderful as that will be, but communion with Christ. At the center of all the worship of heaven is Jesus Christ, in all his glory.

Jonathan Edwards once preached a sermon on the joy of communing with Christ in glory. Edwards was a great preacher during the Great Awakening and perhaps the greatest mind in American history.

The occasion of his sermon was the funeral of David Brainerd (1718–47). It was a sad funeral because Brainerd's brief life had been an inspiration to many Christians. He had served as a pioneer missionary to the Native American Indians of eastern Pennsylvania. After barely a year of riding from place to place on horseback and preaching the gospel, more than one hundred Indians had been converted. But Brainerd contracted a disease and died when he was just twenty-nine years old.

Edwards felt the loss deeply because of the apparent loss to the cause of missions and because of his warm friendship with Brainerd, who died in the Edwards home. Yet as America's greatest theologian delivered his friend's funeral sermon, his sadness was replaced with the joy of eternal communion with Christ:

> We cannot continue always in these earthly tabernacles. They are very frail, and will soon decay and fall. . . . Our souls must soon leave them, and go into the eternal world. O, how infinitely great will be the privilege and happiness of those, who, at that time shall go to be with Christ in his glory . . . where he sits on the throne, as the King of angels, and the God of the universe; shining forth as the Sun of that world of glory;— there to dwell in the full, constant, and everlasting view of his beauty and brightness;—there most freely and intimately to converse with him, and fully to enjoy his love, as his friends and brethren; there to share with him in the infinite pleasure and joy which he has in the enjoyment of his Father—there to sit with him on his throne, to reign with him in the possession of all things . . . and to join with him in joyful songs of praise to his Father and our Father, to his God and our God forever and ever![7]

And all the saints say, "Amen. Come Lord Jesus. Come soon!"

Spiritual Gifts Questionnaire

Introduction

The Spiritual Gifts Questionnaire is designed to identify your spiritual gift(s).* This appendix may be reproduced as needed.

Instructions

For each question below, enter a number in the left-hand blank to indicate whether the question reflects your experience much, some, little, or not at all. Use the following scale:

3 = much   2 = some   1 = little   0 = not at all

_____ 1. Do you feel a great amount of satisfaction performing routine tasks for God's glory?

---

* This previously unpublished inventory is used by permission of Reverend Ronald Steel, who developed it while on staff at Briarwood Presbyterian Church in Birmingham, Alabama. It is based in part on resources from Bill Gothard's Institute in Basic Youth Conflicts and on C. Peter Wagner's *Finding Your Spiritual Gifts: Wagner-Modified Houts Questionnaire* (Glendale, Calif.: Regal, 1995).

_____ 2. Do you have a sensitivity to recognize people's prayer needs before others do?

_____ 3. Do you enjoy public speaking to a group?

_____ 4. Are you able to provide food/lodging graciously to those in need?

_____ 5. Are you effective in persuading others to move toward achieving biblical objectives?

_____ 6. When circumstances are bleak, do you always have the ability to see God keeping his promises to you?

_____ 7. Do you know when and to whom to delegate important responsibility?

_____ 8. Do you seek out unbelievers in order to win them to Christ?

_____ 9. Do you adapt easily to a different culture than your own?

_____ 10. Do you effectively apply biblical truth to your own life?

_____ 11. Do you enjoy assisting leaders so that they can focus their energies on their primary responsibilities?

_____ 12. Do you manage your money well in order to give over and above the tithe to the Lord's work?

_____ 13. Can you clearly and correctly perceive the difference between truth and error immediately when statements are made about spiritual matters?

_____ 14. Have you had the desire to care for the spiritual needs of a group of people?

_____ 15. Have people often expressed to you how much you have encouraged them in time of need?

_____ 16. For your own enjoyment, do you regularly and systematically study God's Word?

_____ 17. When you hear of someone in the hospital, do you feel challenged to go and comfort him or her?

_____ 18. When you hear of a job that needs to be done, are you anxious to do it?

_____ 19. Do you faithfully pray for others, recognizing that their effectiveness as a teacher, employer, husband, wife, etc., depends on it?

_____ 20. Do you find it easy to organize your thoughts and explain things to people?

_____ 21. Can you provide a comfortable haven for guests without the feeling of family interruption?

_____ 22. Do you have a sense of direction in life and see other Christians follow you?

_____ 23. Do you have an unusually strong, personal assurance from God that he will accomplish great things that may seem impossible to others?

_____ 24. Are you able to organize ideas, people, things, and time for more effective ministry?

_____ 25. Do you find it easy to make friends with non-Christian people?

_____ 26. Would you like to learn another language well in order to minister to different peoples?

_____ 27. When you need to make a decision between several biblical alternatives, do you have a clear sense of which one is best?

_____ 28. Do you sense the need to help other people to become more effective in their ministry?

_____ 29. Do you enjoy giving to the Lord's work without asking the question of whether or not you can afford it right now?

_____ 30. Do you accurately recognize whether a teaching is of God, Satan, or human origin?

_____ 31. Do you seek to protect and provide for those under your spiritual care?

_____ 32. Do you find that you are a good and patient listener?

_____ 33. Do you study and read a great deal in order to discover biblical truth?

_____ 34. Do you feel a lot of compassion for those who are suffering physically and think of ways to help them?

_____ 35. Do you enjoy taking care of physical tasks for the church?

_____ 36. Do you pray a lot and enjoy it?

_____ 37. Do you enjoy spending time learning new biblical truths in order to share them with others?

_____ 38. Do you have a knack for making strangers feel at home?

_____ 39. Do you enjoy leading, inspiring, and motivating others to involve themselves in the Lord's work?

_____ 40. Do you find God working in amazing ways when you encounter difficult circumstances?

_____ 41. Are you able to make effective and efficient plans to accomplish goals of the group?

_____ 42. Do you find yourself regularly sharing the gospel message with nonbelievers?

_____ 43. Do you relate well to Christians of different races, languages, or cultures?

_____ 44. Do you have the ability to choose from several biblical alternatives an option that usually works?

_____ 45. Do you enjoy doing routine tasks that lead to more effective ministry by others?

_____ 46. Are you really thrilled when someone asks you to help financially in some project, seeing this as a great honor or privilege?

_____ 47. Can you accurately distinguish between what is good and what is evil?

_____ 48. Do you enjoy the responsibility for the spiritual well-being of a group of Christians?

_____ 49. Do you find yourself urging others to seek a biblical solution to their affliction or suffering?

_____ 50. Does studying the Bible personally come easy for you?

_____ 51. Would you really like a regular ministry to the sick, shut-ins, or others who are hurting?

_____ 52. When someone asks a favor of you, do you feel grateful that they asked you?

_____ 53. Do you see God consistently answer your prayers?

_____ 54. Have you been effective in communicating biblical truths to others, which produce changes in knowledge, attitudes, values, or conduct?

_____ 55. Do you take unexpected guests in stride, without apology for how your house may look?

_____ 56. Have you influenced others to accomplish a particular task or biblical purpose?

_____ 57. Has God done miraculous works for you and others in response to your prayers?

_____ 58. Do you desire to help organize ministry areas and activities?

_____ 59. Can you explain clearly that Jesus Christ is the Savior and see a positive response in your listeners?

_____ 60. Would you enjoy living in a foreign country, not just visiting?

_____ 61. Do you feel an unusual presence of God and personal confidence when important decisions need to be made?

_____ 62. Do you regularly look for ways to relieve leaders of responsibilities that you or others could do?

_____ 63. Do you give consistently and sacrificially to the Lord, knowing he will meet your needs?

_____ 64. Are your perceptions of people's motives always correct?

_____ 65. Do you enjoy the task of relating to the successes and failures of the same group over a long period?

_____ 66. Do you really get a lot of joy encouraging people who are going through personal problems and trials?

_____ 67. Do you have a strong desire to study God's Word?

_____ 68. Have others encouraged you to have a special ministry toward the sick and suffering?

_____ 69. Are you always looking for jobs to do and to get done?

_____ 70. Do you always take prayer requests very seriously?

_____ 71. When you hear a spiritual question, are you anxious to both find and give an answer?

_____ 72. Do you enjoy making your home available to those in the Lord's service for an extended period?

_____ 73. Do others follow you because you have expertise regarding the ministry of the church?

_____ 74. When all looks dim, do you say and do things that demonstrate your confidence in God?

_____ 75. Are you effective in giving direction to and making decisions for others?

_____ 76. Would you like to learn how to share your faith more effectively?

_____ 77. Do you think of the people in other cultures who have never heard of Christ?

_____ 78. Do you enjoy working out solutions to complicated problems?

_____ 79. Would you be happy as a teacher's aide in a Bible class?

_____ 80. Do you look for extra opportunities to give without hearing any appeals?

_____ 81. Do you always see through a person who is a phony before it is evident to others?

_____ 82. Is it important for you to know intimately and be well known by those you serve and guide?

_____ 83. Have you been effective in helping the complacent and redirecting the wayward to face life's reality?

_____ 84. Do people often recognize your ability to distinguish important facts from Scripture?

_____ 85. Do you desire to work with those who have physical or mental problems in order to alleviate their suffering?

_____ 86. Are you able to identify and meet the needs involved in a task in the Lord's work?

_____ 87. Is praying together with and for other Christians very meaningful to you?

_____ 88. Do you desire to teach God's Word regularly?

_____ 89. Can you provide a gracious haven for guests without a great hassle?

_____ 90. Do you usually take the leadership in a group where none exists?

_____ 91. Do you believe God's promises to a greater degree than your Christian friends?

_____ 92. Does planning come easily to you?

_____ 93. Do you share joyfully how Christ has brought you to himself in a way that is meaningful to nonbelievers?

_____ 94. Do you have a strong desire to see peoples of other cultures won to the Lord, and would you like to help?

_____ 95. Do people you recommend for positions regularly prove to be good selections?

_____ 96. Have others involved in ministry sought you out to assist them in some way?

_____ 97. Do you feel deeply moved to give, and do you give, when confronted with urgent financial needs in God's work?

_____ 98. Is it instantly clear to you whether a person is growing or stagnant in his/her spiritual life?

_____ 99. Are you able to restore persons who have wandered away from their Christian community?

_____ 100. Do you enjoy verbally encouraging the wavering, troubled, or discouraged?

_____ 101. Do you regularly acquire and master new facts and principles from your own study of the Bible?

_____ 102. Do you feel strongly that the church should care for those who are hurting and that you would like to help?

_____ 103. Would you enjoy being called upon to do special jobs around the church that no one else will do?

_____104. Do people regularly share prayer requests with you because they know you will pray about them?

_____105. Have other people ever told you that you ought to be teaching on a regular basis?

_____106. Do you enjoy having strangers in your home?

_____107. Do you usually think about long-range goals rather than short-range goals?

_____108. Have you regularly visualized great things for the future of God's work and seen them accomplished?

_____109. Do you like the responsibility for the success or failure of a group or organization?

_____110. Has God used you to lead others to a decision for salvation through faith in Christ?

_____111. Do you make friends easily with people from different cultures?

_____112. Are you able to perceive and apply biblical truth to the specific needs of the body?

_____113. Do you sense great satisfaction for helping someone else become successful?

_____114. Do you give things or money cheerfully and sacrificially to the Lord's work?

_____115. Have you accurately perceived a person under satanic influence?

_____116. Have you been effective helping needy Christians by guiding them to relevant portions of the Bible and praying with them?

_____117. Do people seek you out in order to get God's solution to their problems?

_____118. Do you have the ability to accurately discover new truths from the Bible for yourself?

_____119. Are you patient to spend time with someone who is physically suffering rather than wanting to leave as soon as you can?

Spiritual Gifts Chart

1. After you have answered the 119 questions above, transfer your answers (3, 2, 1, or 0) to the blanks under the question numbers on the chart below.

TOTAL   GIFT

Q. 1   18   35   52   69   86   103
A. __ __   __   __   __   __   __ = ____   SERVICE

Q. 2   19   36   53   70   87   104
A. __ __   __   __   __   __   __ = ____   INTERCESSION

Q. 3   20   37   54   71   88   105
A. __ __   __   __   __   __   __ = ____   TEACHING

Q. 4   21   38   55   72   89   106
A. __ __   __   __   __   __   __ = ____   HOSPITALITY

Q. 5   22   39   56   73   90   107
A. __ __   __   __   __   __   __ = ____   LEADERSHIP

Q. 6   23   40   57   74   91   108
A. __ __   __   __   __   __   __ = ____   FAITH

Q. 7   24   41   58   75   92   109
A. __ __   __   __   __   __   __ = ____   ADMINISTRATION

Q. 8   25   42   59   76   93   110
A. __ __   __   __   __   __   __ = ____   EVANGELISM

Q. 9   26   43   60   77   94   111
A. __ __   __   __   __   __   __ = ____   MISSIONS

Q. 10 27   44   61   78   95   112
A. __ __   __   __   __   __   __ = ____   WISDOM

Q. 11 28 45 62 79 96 113
A. __ __ __ __ __ __ __ = ____   HELPS

Q. 12 29 46 63 80 97 114
A. __ __ __ __ __ __ __ = ____   GIVING

Q. 13 30 47 64 81 98 115
A. __ __ __ __ __ __ __ = ____   DISCERNMENT

Q. 14 31 48 65 82 99 116
A. __ __ __ __ __ __ __ = ____   SHEPHERDING

Q. 15 32 49 66 83 100 117
A. __ __ __ __ __ __ __ = ____   EXHORTATION

Q. 16 33 50 67 84 101 118
A. __ __ __ __ __ __ __ = ____   KNOWLEDGE

Q. 17 34 51 68 85 102 119
A. __ __ __ __ __ __ __ = ____   MERCY

2. Now add together your seven numbers across each answer row and enter the sum in the TOTAL column.

3. Note the three highest rated gifts, and enter them below. Then review the gift definitions that follow. The areas in which you have scored highest provide a tentative evaluation of what your gift(s) may be. This process should either affirm what you already know or provide direction for you to follow as God leads you to use the gifts he has given you.

1. _____

2. _____

3. _____

Definitions and Scripture References

SERVICE. The gift of service is the special ability that God gives to certain members of the body of Christ to identify the unmet needs involved in a task related to God's work and make use of available resources to meet those needs, thus helping accomplish the desired goals. (Rom. 12:7; Eph. 6:5–9)

INTERCESSION. The gift of intercession is the special ability that God gives to certain members of the body of Christ to pray for extended periods of time on a regular basis and see frequent and specific answers to their prayers to a degree much greater than is expected of the average Christian. (Col. 1:9–12; 1 Tim. 2:1–2)

TEACHING. The gift of teaching is the special ability that God gives to certain members of the body of Christ to communicate biblical information relevant to the health and ministry of the body and its members in such a way that others will learn. (Acts 13:1; 18:24–28; Rom. 12:7; 1 Cor. 12:28; Eph. 4:11)

HOSPITALITY. The gift of hospitality is the special ability that God gives to certain members of the body of Christ to provide an open house and warm welcome to those in need of food and lodging. (Acts 16:15; Rom. 12:9–13; Heb. 13:1–2; 1 Peter 4:9).

LEADERSHIP. The gift of leadership is the special ability that God gives to certain members of the body of Christ to set goals in accordance with God's purpose for the future and to communicate those goals to others in such a way that they voluntarily and harmoniously work together to accomplish those goals for the glory of God. (Acts 15:7–12; Rom. 12:8; 1 Tim. 5:17)

FAITH. The gift of faith is the special ability that God gives to certain members of the body of Christ to discern with extraordinary confidence the will and purposes of God for the future of his work. (Acts 11:22–24; 27:21–25; 1 Cor. 12:9)

ADMINISTRATION. The gift of administration is the special ability that God gives to certain members of the body of Christ to understand clearly the immediate and long-range goals of a particular unit of the body of Christ and to devise and execute effective plans for the accomplishment of those goals. (Acts 6:1–7; 1 Cor. 12:28).

EVANGELISM. The gift of evangelism is the special ability that God gives to certain members of the body of Christ to share the gospel with unbelievers in such a way that men and women become Jesus' disciples and responsible members of the body of Christ. (Acts 8:5; 6:26–40; 21:8; Eph. 4:11; 2 Tim. 4:5)

MISSIONS. The gift of missions is the special ability that God gives to certain members of the body of Christ to minister by means of whatever other spiritual gifts they have in a second culture. (Acts 8:4–5; 13:2–3; 22:21; 1 Cor. 9:19–23; Eph. 3:7–8)

WISDOM. The gift of wisdom is the special ability that God gives to certain members of the body of Christ to know the mind of the Holy Spirit in such a way as to receive insight into how given knowledge may best be applied to specific needs arising in the body of Christ. (Acts 6:3, 10; 1 Cor. 12:8; James 1:5–6; 2 Peter 3:15)

HELPS. The gift of helps is the special ability that God gives to certain members of the body of Christ to invest the talents they have in the life and ministry of other members of the body, thus enabling them to increase the effectiveness of their spiritual gifts. (Rom. 16:1–2; 1 Cor. 12:28)

GIVING. The gift of giving is the special ability that God gives to certain members of the body of Christ to contribute their material resources to the work of the Lord with liberality and cheerfulness. (Luke 21:4; Acts 4:34; 2 Cor. 9:7)

DISCERNMENT. The gift of discernment is the special ability that God gives to certain members of the body of Christ to know with assurance whether certain behavior purported to be of God is in reality divine, human, or satanic. (Acts 16:16–18; 1 Cor. 12:10; 1 John 4:1–6)

SHEPHERDING. The gift of shepherding is the special ability that God gives to certain members of the body of Christ to assume a long-term personal responsibility for the spiritual welfare of a group of believers. (Eph. 4:11; 1 Thess. 5:12; 1 Tim. 3:1–7)

EXHORTATION. The gift of exhortation is the special ability that God gives to certain members of the body of Christ to minister words of comfort, consolation, encouragement, and counsel to other members of the body in such a way that they feel helped and healed. (Acts 14:22; Rom. 12:8; 1 Tim. 4:13; Heb. 10:25)

KNOWLEDGE. The gift of knowledge is the special ability that God gives to certain members of the body of Christ to discover, accumulate, analyze, and clarify information and ideas that are pertinent to the growth and well-being of the body. (1 Cor. 12:8)

MERCY. The gift of mercy is the special ability that God gives to certain members of the body of Christ to feel genuine empathy and compassion for individuals, both Christian and non-Christian, who suffer distressing physical, mental, or emotional problems, and to translate that compassion into cheerfully done deeds that reflect Christ's love and alleviate the suffering. (Matt. 5:7; Acts 16:33–34; Rom. 12:8; Heb. 4:16)

Notes

Preface

1 Robert D. Putnam, *Bowling Alone: The Collapse and Revival of American Community* (New York: Simon & Schuster, 2000).
2 Charles Colson and Ellen Santilli Vaughn, *The Body* (Dallas: Word, 1992), 32.
3 Dietrich Bonhoeffer, *Life Together*, trans. John W. Doberstein (San Francisco: Harper & Row, 1954), 20.

Chapter 1: What Is the Communion of Saints?

1 John Winthrop, quoted in Perry Miller and Thomas H. Johnson, eds., *The Puritans*, rev. ed., 2 vols. (New York: Harper, 1963), 1:197–98.
2 Philip Schaff, *The Creeds of Christendom*, 3 vols. (Grand Rapids: Baker, 1993), 1:55.
3 The early development of Catholic sainthood is traced in J. N. D. Kelly, *Early Christian Doctrines*, rev. ed. (New York: Harper & Row, 1978), 490–91.
4 Martin Luther, *The Large Catechism* (Philadelphia: Fortress, 1959), 60–61.
5 James Bannerman, *The Church of Christ: A Treatise on the Nature, Powers, Ordinances, Discipline and Government of the Christian Church*, 2 vols. (1869; repr. London: Banner of Truth, 1974), 1:91–92.
6 Zacharias Ursinus, *Commentary on the Heidelberg Catechism* (Philadelphia: P&R, 1956), 305.
7 Johan Heidegger, *Medulla Theologiae Christianae* (Zurich, 1696), 26.7, quoted in Heinrich Heppe, *Reformed Dogmatics*, rev. and ed. Ernst Bizer, trans. G. T. Thomson (Grand Rapids: Baker, 1978), 659.
8 Luther, *The Large Catechism*, 61.
9 Ursinus, *Commentary on the Heidelberg Catechism*, 303.
10 Dietrich Bonhoeffer, *The Communion of Saints: A Dogmatic Inquiry into the Sociology of the Church* (New York: Harper & Row, 1963), 42.

Notes

11 James Montgomery Boice, *Two Cities, Two Loves* (Downers Grove, Ill.: Inter-Varsity Press, 1996), 247.

12 Alexis de Tocqueville, *Democracy in America*, 2 vols. (New Rochelle, N.Y.: Arlington House, 1965), 2:106.

Chapter 2: Union with Christ

1 Johan Heidegger, *Medulla Theologiae Christianae* (Zurich, 1696), 26.7, quoted in Heinrich Heppe, *Reformed Dogmatics*, rev. and ed. Ernst Bizer, trans. G. T. Thomson (Grand Rapids: Baker, 1978), 659.

2 John MacArthur Jr., *The Church: The Body of Christ* (Panorama City, Calif.: Word of Grace, 1981), 51.

3 John Murray, *Redemption Accomplished and Applied* (Grand Rapids: Eerdmans, 1955), 161.

4 John Calvin, *Institutes of the Christian Religion*, trans. Ford Lewis Battles, 2 vols., Library of Christian Classics 20–21 (Philadelphia: Westminster, 1960), 3.1.1.

5 Sinclair B. Ferguson, *The Christian Life: A Doctrinal Introduction* (Edinburgh: Banner of Truth, 1989), 105.

6 Obadiah Sedgwick, *The Bowels of Tender Mercy Sealed in the Everlasting Covenant* (London, 1661), 63.

7 Thomas Boston, *Human Nature in Its Fourfold State* (Edinburgh: Banner of Truth, 1989), 282–83.

8 Anthony A. Hoekema, *Saved by Grace* (Grand Rapids: Eerdmans, 1989), 54.

9 Murray, *Redemption Accomplished and Applied*, 165.

10 Calvin, *Institutes*, 4.1.2.

11 A. A. Hodge, *The Confession of Faith* (1869; repr. Edinburgh: Banner of Truth, 1969), 324.

Chapter 3: Baptized into Communion

1 John Calvin, *Institutes of the Christian Religion*, trans. Ford Lewis Battles, 2 vols., Library of Christian Classics 20–21 (Philadelphia: Westminster, 1960), 4.15.1.

Chapter 4: Members Only

1 Dietrich Bonhoeffer, *The Cost of Discipleship* (London: SCM, 1959), 218.

2 G. I. Williamson, *The Westminster Confession of Faith for Study Classes* (Philadelphia: P&R, 1964), 188.

3 *The Book of Church Order of the Presbyterian Church in America*, 5th ed. (Atlanta: Office of the Stated Clerk of the General Assembly of the Presbyterian Church in America, 1998), 27–1.

4 Ibid., 27–4.

5 G. Eric Lane, *Members One of Another* (London: Evangelical Press, 1968), 18.

6 Augustine of Hippo *Enchiridion* 17.65.

7 John Calvin, *Institutes of the Christian Religion*, trans. Ford Lewis Battles, 2 vols., Library of Christian Classics 20–21 (Philadelphia: Westminster, 1960), 4.1.4.

8 Charles Colson and Ellen Santilli Vaughn, *The Body* (Dallas: Word, 1992), 32.

9 D. Martyn Lloyd-Jones, *Knowing the Times* (Edinburgh: Banner of Truth, 1989), 30.

Chapter 5: United in Love

1 Augustine, *The Literal Meaning of Genesis*, trans. John Hammond Taylor (New York: Newman, 1982), 11.15.20.

2 Martin Luther, *The Large Catechism* (Philadelphia: Fortress, 1959), 61.

3 Richard Sibbes, *Works*, 6 vols. (Edinburgh, 1862–64), 3:433.

4 The course of their rivalry is traced in Myrick Land, *The Fine Art of Literary Mayhem* (Lanham, Md.: Lexikos, 1983), 82–109.

5 Francis A. Schaeffer, *The Mark of the Christian* (Downers Grove, Ill.: InterVarsity Press, 1970), 17–18.

Chapter 6: Assembly Required

1 John Wesley, quoted in J. I. Packer, *God's Words: Studies of Key Bible Themes* (Downers Grove, Ill.: InterVarsity Press, 1981), 199.

2 Gene Getz, *Praying for One Another* (Wheaton, Ill.: Victor, 1982), 11.

3 Robert Harris, *A Treatise of the New Covenant* (1632), quoted in William Barker, *Puritan Profiles* (Fearn, Ross-shire: Christian Focus, 1996), 165.

4 Pliny, quoted in *Glimpses*, Christian History Institute, no. 25.

5 Spiros Zodhiates, *The Lord's Prayer*, rev. ed. (Chattanooga, Tenn.: AMG, 1991), 46.

6 Justin Martyr, "The First Apology of Justin, the Martyr," trans. Edward Rochie Hardy, in *Early Christian Fathers*, ed. Cyril C. Richardson (New York: Macmillan, 1970), 225–89 (quote, 287).

Chapter 7: The Communion Table

1 Thomas Boston, *The Complete Works of the Late Rev. Thomas Boston of Ettrick*, ed. Samuel M'Millan, 12 vols. (1853; repr. Wheaton, Ill.: Richard Owen Roberts, 1980), 8:218–19.

2 John Calvin, *Institutes of the Christian Religion*, trans. Ford Lewis Battles, 2 vols., Library of Christian Classics 20–21 (Philadelphia: Westminster, 1960), 4.17.33.
3 Ibid., 4.17.32.
4 G. Johnstone Ross, quoted in Donald Macleod, *Presbyterian Worship: Its Meaning and Method* (Richmond: John Knox, 1965), 68.

Chapter 8: Gifts and Graces

1 See John Bunyan, *The Pilgrim's Progress* (New York: New American Library, 1964), 22–23.
2 George W. Bethune, *Expository Lectures on the Heidelberg Catechism* (New York: Sheldon, 1864), 76.
3 Ray C. Stedman, *Body Life* (Glendale, Calif.: Regal, 1972), 40.
4 Zacharias Ursinus, *Commentary on the Heidelberg Catechism* (Philadelphia: P&R, 1956), 304.
5 Clement, "The Epistles of Clement," trans. and ed. John Keith, in *The Gospel of Peter, The Diatessaron of Tatian . . . The Epistles of Clement, Origen's Commentary on John and Matthew,* ed. Allan Menzies, Ante-Nicene Fathers, 10 vols. (1896; repr. Peabody, Mass.: Hendrickson, 1994), 9:225–56 (quote, 240).
6 John Owen, *Works*, 16 vols. (1850–1853; repr. Edinburgh: Banner of Truth, 1965), 9:267.

Chapter 9: Relief in Outward Things

1 John Calvin, *Sermons on Deuteronomy* (1583; repr. Edinburgh: Banner of Truth, 1987), 252.
2 Jerry Bridges, *The Crisis of Caring* (Phillipsburg, N.J.: P&R, 1985), 132.
3 C. Van Dam, "Some Old Testament Roots and Their Continued Signficance," *Reformed Servant*, vol. 1, no. 1, 17.
4 Charles Hodge, *A Commentary on the Second Epistle to the Corinthians* (London: Banner of Truth, 1959), 133.
5 Matthew Henry, *Commentary on the Whole Bible*, 6 vols. (New York: Fleming H. Revell, n.d.), 5: n.p.
6 Herman Witsius, *Sacred Dissertations on What Is Commonly Called the Apostles' Creed*, 2 vols. (1823; repr. Escondido, Calif.: Den Dulk Christian Foundation, 1993), 2:383.
7 Cotton Mather, *The Diary of Cotton Mather, 1709–1724*, ed. Kenneth Murdock, 2 vols. (New York: Frederick Unger, 1971), 2:48, 77, 80, 113, 213.

Chapter 10: Mutual Edification

1 J. I. Packer, *God's Words: Studies of Key Bible Themes* (Downers Grove, Ill.: InterVarsity Press, 1981), 193.

2 John Calvin, *Sermons on Deuteronomy* (1583; repr. Edinburgh: Banner of Truth, 1987), 237.

3 John Calvin, *Institutes of the Christian Religion*, trans. Ford Lewis Battles, 2 vols., Library of Christian Classics 20–21 (Philadelphia: Westminster, 1960), 4.12.1.

4 Richard Baxter, in *A Grief Sanctified: Passing Through Grief to Peace and Joy*, ed. J. I. Packer (Ann Arbor, Mich.: Servant, 1997), 104.

5 Ibid., 121.

6 See William Williams, *The Experience Meeting* (London: Evangelical Press, 1973).

7 George Whitefield, quoted in John R. W. Stott, *One People: Laymen and Clergy in God's Church* (Downers Grove, Ill.: InterVarsity Press, 1971), 88.

8 Cotton Mather, *The Diary of Cotton Mather, 1681–1707*, ed. Kenneth Murdock, 2 vols. (New York: Frederick Unger, 1971), 1:239–40.

9 Esther Edwards, quoted in Iain Murray, *Jonathan Edwards: A New Biography* (Edinburgh: Banner of Truth, 1987), 406.

10 Dietrich Bonhoeffer, *Life Together*, trans. John W. Doberstein (San Francisco: Harper & Row, 1954), 86.

Chapter 11: All in the Family

1 Martin Luther King Jr., *Where Do We Go from Here: Chaos or Community?* (Boston: Beacon, 1967), 28.

2 Manuel Ortiz, *One New People: Models for Developing a Multiethnic Church* (Downers Grove, Ill.: InterVarsity Press, 1996), 135.

3 Donald Grey Barnhouse, *Eternity* (March 1961), 27.

Chapter 12: Worldwide Communion

1 Tom Sine, quoted in C. John Miller, *Powerful Evangelism for the Powerless*, rev. ed. (Phillipsburg, N.J.: P&R, 1997), 68.

2 Kenneth Scott Latourette, quoted in Ernest Trice Thompson, *Through the Ages: A History of the Christian Church* (Richmond: Covenant Life, 1965), 21.

3 Herman Witsius, *Sacred Dissertations on What Is Commonly Called the Apostles' Creed*, 2 vols. (1823; repr. Escondido, Calif.: Den Dulk Christian Foundation, 1993), 2:381–82.

4 Nina Shea, *In the Lion's Den* (Nashville: Broadman & Holman, 1997), 1.

5 David C. Barrett, "Annual Statistical Table on Global Mission: 1997," *International Bulletin of Missionary Research* (January 1997), 25.

6 David C. Barrett, *World Christian Encyclopedia*, quoted in *Prism* (January/February 1997), 17.

Chapter 13: For All the Saints

1 John Owen, *Meditations and Discourses Concerning the Glory of Christ* (London, 1691), 5.

2 Thomas Boston, *Human Nature in Its Fourfold State* (Edinburgh: Banner of Truth, 1989), 452–53.

3 Sinclair B. Ferguson, *The Christian Life: A Doctrinal Introduction* (Edinburgh: Banner of Truth, 1989), 194.

4 Boston, *Human Nature in Its Fourfold State*, 446.

5 C. S. Lewis, *The Latin Letters of C. S. Lewis*, trans. and ed. Martin Moynihan (Wheaton, Ill.: Crossway, 1987), 48.

6 Richard Baxter, *The Saints' Everlasting Rest* (London, 1650), 81.

7 Jonathan Edwards, *Jonathan Edwards: Representative Selections* (New York: Hill and Wang, 1935), 173–74.

Leader's Guide

Chapter 1: What Is the Communion of the Saints?

Chapter Summary
God created us with a hunger for deep spiritual communion with one another. His provision for this hunger is a living fellowship of love, centered in Jesus Christ, a fellowship that happens in the communion of saints. The communion of saints may be defined as the living fellowship of all true believers, who are united in love by their union with Christ and have spiritual communion with one another as they share in corporate worship, spiritual gifts, Christian graces, material goods, and mutual edification.

Objective
Your goal as class leader is to present a biblical picture of the communion of saints.

Lesson
I. The fellowship of believers is of the utmost importance to God. It is the means he has ordained for many spiritual blessings. To illuminate this truth, ask someone in the class to read aloud Ephesians 2:19–20. Then build a discussion from the following questions:

1. How do believers together become a holy temple in the Lord?
2. According to this passage, what is the purpose for which we are being built together?

II. The apostle Paul typically ended his epistles to the churches with personal greetings and a pastoral benediction. Paul had a deep sense of the importance of the communion of saints, and it comes through in his personal remarks about the spiritual blessings that flow from fellowship. Ask class members to read aloud the following passages from Paul's letters, and after each one, discuss the following questions:

2 Corinthians 13:11–14

1. In verse 11, what four things does Paul instruct the Corinthian believers to do?
2. What blessing accompanies conformity to his instructions?
3. According to verse 12, how are the saints in Corinth to greet one another? What do you think was Paul's intention behind this sort of greeting? Define a modern-day equivalent to Paul's type of greeting.
4. Notice in verse 13 that Paul sends greetings from another body of believers. How does your church create fellowship with other churches in your city and around the world?
5. What three blessings does Paul send to the believers in verse 14? How would individual believers at Corinth have heard Paul's letter and thus been able to receive those blessings?

Ephesians 6:21–22

1. For what purpose does Paul send Tychicus to the church in Ephesus? What does this teach about the significance of fellowship with believers outside our church?

1 Thessalonians 5:23–28

1. According to verse 25, what is one important component in the communion of saints?

2. Paul charged the believers at Thessalonica to read his letter to all local believers. Discuss what his charge reveals about the importance of believers gathering together.

Activity

End this lesson by brainstorming some ways to deepen communion among the believers in your church. Begin the discussion by naming several ways in which the members of your congregation work together to enable spiritual fellowship. Are there midweek Bible studies? How about opportunities for neighborhood outreach? Does your church promote ministries to those in need? What about support for missionaries? In addition to the Sunday worship services, are there other times when the congregation gathers together? Perhaps your discussion will reveal a need for greater fellowship. Before ending the lesson, have the group come up with at least one idea to increase opportunities for communion. Discuss the possibilities of a churchwide picnic in summertime or an evening of caroling just before Christmas. Make plans to present your idea to the elders or to your pastor.

Chapter 2: Union with Christ

Chapter Summary

Jesus Christ is the thread that ties all believers together. Apart from him there is no true communion. Union with Christ comes before our union with one another. In fact, union with Christ is the definition of what it means to be a Christian. Through Christ, we together share all the privileges provided through this union. Union with Christ is a life-giving relationship. It is also an intimate, exclusive, and passionate covenant. The believer's union with Christ, therefore, is not a private relationship. It is lived out in fellowship with other believers. We cannot be united to Christ without being united to every other Christian. We are all in Christ together.

Objective

Your goal as class leader is to help the group understand their union with Christ and why this union is the foundation for communion with all other Christians.

Lesson

What is it like to be united to Christ? Chapter 2 illustrates the answer using examples of this union found in Scripture. From John's Gospel we learn that our union with Christ is likened to a branch growing from a vine. The Bible also shows us how union with Christ functions like the parts of a human body, the institution of marriage, a covenant, a household, and a building. By taking a deeper look at some of those examples, you can largely accomplish your objective for this lesson.

I. Ask someone to read aloud John 15:1–8. Then begin a discussion with the following questions:

1. Why is it vital to remain united to Christ?
2. What can a believer accomplish apart from Christ?
3. What happens when the branch and vine are not joined?
4. According to verse 8, what is the outcome of abiding in Christ?
5. What sort of relationship do you think is indicated by this illustration? In your discussion, be sure that the following key points are mentioned:
   a. Our relationship with Christ is a living relationship.
   b. Christ is the source of our vitality.

II. Our union with Christ is like the workings of a human body. This illustration is a good one to discuss because there are some Christians who feel that their limited abilities leave them with little to contribute to the communion of saints. Looking at 1 Corinthians 12:12–27 will help the class to see that every individual believer is necessary for the truest possible communion. Ask someone to read the passage aloud. Then talk through the following questions:

1. What do verses 15–19 teach about how the uniqueness of each believer builds unity?
2. Consider the diversity of functions and offices within your church congregation. There are many, including pastors, elders, the diaconate, the clean-up crew, nursery attendants, and those who set up for coffee hour. Discuss how each one is necessary for your church to function well. Can you see God's providence in bringing together such a diverse group of people?

III. Union with Christ is also likened to marriage. The sanctity of marriage has suffered in contemporary culture, but God's standard for this institution remains one of lifelong commitment and deep intimacy. Marriage as God intended is a picture of our union with Christ. Have someone read Ephesians 5:32–33. Then ask the class to answer the questions that follow:

1. Name all the ways that Christ acts in the role of husband to believers.
2. What two things are believers to do in their role as the bride of Christ?
3. How is the love of Christ like that of a husband's love toward his wife?
4. Who takes on the greater responsibility in this spiritual marriage?

Activity

Union with Christ entails union with every other believer. Ask each member of the class to reach out to someone sitting alone in church this Sunday or to someone who frequently heads for the door during the final hymn. Encourage the class to invite this loner to coffee hour or their small group Bible study. Even a brief conversation can reveal particular needs or interests someone may have, and if such needs are detected, the individual can be introduced to an appropriate ministry leader.

Chapter 3: Baptized into Communion

Chapter Summary

The saints enter union with Christ through baptism. We are also united to one another through baptism. This sacrament signifies and confirms that we belong to Christ and to his community. Baptism is a sign of our commitment to Christ as Lord, but it is primarily a sign of God's promise to us. It is an outward and physical sign of an inward and spiritual grace. Baptism does not merely signify; it also seals. Receiving baptism brings to us the benefits of the covenant, which include the communion of saints.

Objective

Your goal as class leader is to convey an understanding of baptism as a sign and seal of God's covenant.

Lesson

I. The answers to the questions below are found in chapter 3. Pose the questions to the class, and generate a discussion from the resulting answers.

1. What does baptism symbolize?
2. How does chapter 3 define a biblical type?

3. What three Old Testament types point forward to baptism into Christ?

4. Why is baptism called a sacrament?

5. What is the connection between Old Testament circumcision and New Testament baptism?

6. How does baptism seal a believer?

7. What are some of the covenant benefits received through baptism?

II. Interpretation of Christian baptism has been widely and hotly debated throughout church history. In fact, baptism is in part responsible for the formation of denominations within the true church. As the class leader, you may encounter those in your class whose views on baptism differ from what is taught in *The Communion of Saints*. Now is a good time in the lesson to ask for questions or comments. Although baptism cannot give salvation to anyone, it usually accompanies salvation, and receiving the sacrament is an act of obedience to God. If questions or disagreements arise, ask volunteers to read aloud the following passages to help clarify Scripture's teaching on baptism: Romans 6:3–8; 1 Corinthians 10:1–2; Colossians 2:11–12; 1 Peter 3:21.

After the passages have been read, suggest that class members spend time in the week ahead rereading them and praying for a deeper understanding of Christian baptism.

III. Ask the class to recount their unique baptism experiences. What do people remember, either from their own baptism or from the baptism of others? Since receiving baptism, is there an awareness of the covenant blessings mentioned in chapter 3?

Activity

In closing, suggest the following resources on Christian baptism for anyone in need of a greater understanding of this sacrament:

1. Westminster Larger Catechism, questions 161–67.
2. Westminster Confession of Faith, chapter 28.
3. Louis Berkhof, *Systematic Theology* (Grand Rapids, Eerdmans, 1941), part 5: The Means of Grace, sections 3 and 4.
4. John P. Sartelle, *Infant Baptism* (Phillipsburg, N.J.: P&R 1985).

Chapter 4: Members Only

Chapter Summary

The communion of saints is for church members only. If you are a believer, failing to join a church can be costly because it hinders the communion of saints. The main task of the church is to gather and perfect the saints, so when Christians join, they receive all the benefits that a true church provides. These include the teaching of God's Word, administration of the sacraments, and spiritual discipline. Joining a church is crucial for Christian growth.

Objective

Your goal as class leader is to show that church membership has its basis in Scripture and that it is necessary for the true communion of saints.

Lesson

I. This chapter on church membership likened the church to a household. Begin the class by asking several people to describe a typical household. Who are its residents? How does each one function within the house? What goes on among family members all living under the same roof? What goals typically unify a household? Why is a household a good analogy for the communion of saints?

Now ask someone to read aloud Ephesians 2:19–22. Then guide a discussion using the following questions:

1. How should each believer see himself or herself in the household of God?
2. What is the undergirding strength of God's household?
3. How does the household grow into a temple?
4. For what purpose are believers built up into a household?

II. Ask a class member to read aloud Acts 2:41–47. Then generate a discussion with the following questions:

1. Chapter 4 describes the mission of the church and the means for fulfilling its mission. Those means are the reading and teaching of God's Word and the administration of the sacraments. Which of those do you find in Acts 2? How were they effective?
2. Acts 2:44 states that the members of that church "had all things in common." Discuss how this relates to the communion of saints. Look through the entire passage again and note the attitude toward church involvement held by those believers. What do you observe?

Activity

How does your church encourage membership? Is there a regular membership class? If so, is it heavily promoted? How are new members publicly welcomed? Ask for volunteers to help out on a membership campaign. Speak to your elder or pastor about creating some flyers or posters for the church bulletin board promoting the next class. If your church doesn't already host one, suggest a new members' reception. As a class, offer to provide refreshments for the reception and clean up afterwards.

Chapter 5: United in Love

Chapter Summary

Love is the primary mark of life in Christ. It is found most frequently and genuinely in the communion of saints. True communion is active, not passive. We must seek to prevent conflict with humility, forgiveness, and love. Seeking reconciliation is love in action. Christian love is much more than a feeling. It involves practical application in the church. Because we are all united in love to Jesus Christ, we must seek the best for all the saints at all times.

Objective

Your goal as class leader is to show how active love among the saints glorifies God and blesses all believers.

Lesson

I. The Bible shows us that conflict can either destroy or strengthen. Acts 15 gives us an example of conflict resolution among disagreeing saints. The issue at hand was circumcision. A disagreement arose among the early believers about whether circumcision was necessary for the communion of saints. Ask a class member to read aloud Acts 15:1–32. Then generate a discussion from the following questions:

1. In seeking to resolve the conflict, what step is initiated in Acts 15:2?
2. What do you discover about Christian conflict resolution in Acts 15:6?
3. How does the apostle Peter address the group in Acts 15:7?
4. In Acts 15:12–13, what approach was taken to facilitate resolution?
5. What was the focus of the arguments presented during that council?

6. After an agreement was reached, what step did the church leaders take to foster churchwide unity about this issue?

II. Chapter 5 points out the apostle Paul's instructions for avoiding conflict among the saints (Eph. 4). Ask the class to open their Bibles to Ephesians 4, and discuss the following questions:

1. Where in your church do you see examples of humility, gentleness, patience, and tolerance? Ask for specific examples.
2. From Ephesians 4:15–16, how does love grow within the church?
3. Discuss some practical ways to prevent anger from festering.
4. From this passage, what sort of talk is necessary to promote love? List the traits you find here that make for uplifting conversation.

Activity

Is there a topic currently in public conflict within your congregation? If so, what steps are being taken to bring resolution? Is there evidence of the Acts 15 model (gathering together, listening and speaking in turn, and emphasizing the principles in Scripture)? Close the class by praying that the current conflict would be resolved in a God-glorifying way and one that deepens the love among the saints in your fellowship.

Chapter 6: Assembly Required

Chapter Summary

Why is weekly church attendance so important? It is crucial because Christian worship is a coming together of a sacred assembly for the purpose of glorifying God. True worship services include the reading and preaching of God's Word, prayer, feasting, and fellowship. Meeting together for worship is necessary for our spiritual growth. When the saints gather on the first day of the week to sing, pray, participate in the Lord's Supper, and to have fellowship with one another, they are enjoying the best of the communion of saints.

Objective

Your goal as class leader is to help the class grasp the necessity of participating with other believers in Christ-centered worship.

Lesson

I. Chapter 6 points out that the biblical model for true worship includes four things. The first is the reading and teaching of God's Word. Then there is the fellowship of the saints. Another is the sacrament of the Lord's Supper. The final element in all true worship is prayer. Discuss how your church exhibits these four characteristics of worship during Sunday services.

II. The importance of communal worship is not stressed in all churches or among all believers. That is likely due to two things: the influence of our humanistic culture and a lack of knowledge of what true worship entails. Address the discussion points that follow:

1. What reasons do people give for not attending church regularly? What did you learn in chapter 6 that could be used to counter those reasons?
2. Name some wrong motivations for attending weekly worship services.
3. Based on the Scripture passages that provide models for Christian worship on the Lord's Day, do you think it is biblical for a church to hold an extra service on another day of the week (to cut down on sanctuary overflow on Sunday, for example, or to accommodate those who can't attend worship on Sunday)? Why or why not?

4. A popular model for church growth today is the seeker-sensitive approach. Seeker-sensitive churches attempt to structure the worship activities to appeal to people who are uncomfortable participating in traditional worship. Based on what you learned from chapter 6 about true worship, identify both the good intentions in this approach and its potential problems.

Activity

Chapter 6 explained that feasting together, sharing a common meal, is a way of sealing the unity of the covenant community. Work together as a class to organize a meal within the fellowship of your congregation. If your church does not hold at least one annual congregational dinner, speak to your elders about getting one started. Volunteer to help! Whether you plan to organize a churchwide meal or a smaller gathering for a particular fellowship group, offer to coordinate the details and meal preparation. When the feast takes place, work together as a class to set the tables, serve the meal, and clean up afterwards.

Chapter 7: The Communion Table

Chapter Summary

The sacrament of the Lord's Supper was instituted by Christ as a demonstration of God's love for us. Our fellowship both with Christ and with one another is deepened as we participate in this holy meal. The Lord's Supper is also called Communion. This title is an indicator that believers are meant to share in the sacrament with one another. It is something we share. The Lord's Supper should always be observed according to the pattern God established in Scripture. Our worship at the Lord's Table advances our communion with God and with one another.

Objective

Your goal as class leader is to help the class understand the deep significance of and blessings that accompany the proper partaking of the Lord's Supper on a regular basis.

Lesson

I. Chapter 7 explains the necessity of participating in the Lord's Supper in a worthy manner; however, such worthiness springs from an understanding of our unworthiness due to sin. Those who partake in communion must come with honesty about their sins, as well as a resolve to repent no matter what the personal cost. Ask someone to read aloud 1 Corinthians 11:27–32. Then, focusing on the seriousness of Paul's exhortation, open a discussion on practical ways to practice self-examination prior to entering into the Communion service.

II. During the Communion service, we may notice someone who is not participating. Discuss possible ways to approach such individuals after the service. How can we show love and the compassion of Christ to them?

III. Lead a discussion from the following questions, covering as many as time permits:

1. How frequently should the Lord's Supper be observed, and what leads you to your conclusion?
2. Name the essential parts of a Communion service.
3. Who should participate in the Lord's Supper, and how should those not invited to partake be encouraged to abstain?
4. For missionaries and other saints in a situation where a makeshift Communion service is the only way to observe the sacrament, may other beverages be substituted for wine or grape juice? What about other solid food in place of the bread? Discuss the significance of the bread and the wine. You may wish to

refer to Matthew 26:26–29; Mark 14:22–25; Luke 22:14–21; 1 Corinthians 11:17–34.

5. How old must a believer be in order to begin partaking of the Lord's Supper?

6. When, if ever, should a member in good standing of a Bible-centered church abstain from participating in the Lord's Supper?

III. If your church is celebrating the Lord's Supper today, close the discussion with a time of prayer in preparation to receive the sacrament.

Activity

Chapter 7 discussed different views on how the Lord's Supper has been understood down through church history. The Roman Catholic doctrine of transubstantiation is one view. Another was the view held by Martin Luther known as consubstantiation. Ulrich Zwingli saw Communion as a memorial service that looked back to Christ's suffering and sacrifice. John Calvin believed in the real spiritual presence of Christ in the sacrament.

Ask for four volunteers from the class who will each be responsible for making an outline of the points in one of the views named above. If the volunteers would like to do more research, your church library may prove helpful, or suggest that they borrow a resource from the pastor. Ask the volunteers to bring their outlines to the next class. When all four have been compiled, ask for another helper to photocopy and distribute the outlines to each class member.

Chapter 8: Gifts and Graces

Chapter Summary

Every Christian has one or more gifts given by the Holy Spirit for the purpose of building up the whole body of Christ. Spiritual gifts and graces are loans to the church from God's unconditional kindness. A grace is an attitude or disposition, whereas a gift is a capacity for service. Some gifts are closely related to natural talents, yet spiritual gifts differ from talents in that they are only for Christians and they are only to be used for spiritual purposes. Gifts and graces are necessary for the advancement of God's kingdom. His purpose in giving them is for the communion of saints. There is a diversity of gifts so that we can all make some contribution to the work of the body.

Objective

Your goal as class leader is to equip the group to seek and discover their personal gifts and graces and to foster an understanding of how those gifts contribute to the communion of saints.

Lesson

I. Ask a class member to read aloud Ephesians 4:7–16. Then begin a discussion with the following questions:

1. According to verse 12, for what purpose are spiritual gifts given to the saints?
2. Based on verse 13, what is the intended goal in exercising our gifts?
3. When spiritual gifts are exercised, what danger is averted?
4. What does verse 16 teach about spiritual gifts and the communion of saints?

II. Answer and discuss the following questions:

1. How many in the class have already identified their spiritual gifts?
2. By what means were those gifts discovered?
3. In what ways have these gifts been confirmed over time?

212

4. In what specific ways are class members exercising their particular gifts in your church?
5. Why is it important for a diversity of gifts to be used in the church?

Activity

Chapter 8 points out the importance of recognizing our personal spiritual gifts. We learn what our gifts are through godly and wise counsel, prayer, and personal desire. One of the most important aspects of identifying our gifts is being open to receiving whatever God sees fit to give us. This is why a full surrender to God of our entire person is necessary before being able to know and exercise our gifts. Periodic gift assessments are also important. Therefore, whether or not you know your gifts, take time to fill out the Spiritual Gifts Questionnaire in the appendix of this book (feel free to make copies). If class time is limited, instruct the class to complete the test at home and bring the results back to the next class for discussion.

Chapter 9: Relief in Outward Things

Chapter Summary

To love God is to have compassion for others. Unless we are helping to relieve our neighbors' material needs, we are not maintaining our communion with the saints. Relief in outward things is not voluntary. It is a manifestation of God's grace in our lives. Charity extends the compassion of Christ to people's deepest needs, and since the deepest needs are always spiritual, relief demands personal involvement. Sharing with the needy strengthens the communion of saints.

Objective

Your goal as class leader is to emphasize why reaching out in specific ways to the needy glorifies God and deepens the communion of saints.

Lesson

I. Scripture teaches that God has great compassion for the least in human society. Ask for volunteers to read aloud Deuteronomy 10:18–19; Psalm 146:9; Matthew 25:31–40; and James 1:27. Point out to the class that in ancient Israel, the family unit was the strength of society. Husbands and fathers were responsible for providing for everyone in their households. That included extended family members, slaves, and servants. Therefore widows and others left alone were placed in perilous positions and were often social outcasts. There were no orphanages or welfare checks to assist those left outside of a family structure.

1. Who are the needy singled out in these passages?
2. What reasons are given for why we should welcome the stranger?
3. How is God glorified when we extend love to the unlovely?
4. How is caring for the needy an act of love toward God?
5. Who are the widows, orphans, and strangers in our society?
6. Based on the teaching in these passages, why do you think James includes the care of the needy in his definition of true religion?

II. Galatians 6:10 instructs, "Therefore, as we have opportunity, let us do good to all, especially to those who are of the household of faith." From Paul's exhortation, we see that relieving the needy takes us beyond our immediate circle of family and friends and brings the love of Christ to the world around us. Discuss the specific ways your church provides for those in need. Include activities that reach out, not only within your own church family, but also to the surrounding community.

III. Ask someone to read aloud 1 John 3:16–18. Then discuss the following points:

1. What happens when we close our hearts to the needs of the saints?
2. This passage is specifically addressed to those who have the world's goods. Name everything that "worldly goods" can possibly include.

Activity

Set a date when the class can work together to help the needy. To determine your specific activity, look first within your congregation. Is there an event already established, perhaps an outreach to the poor or homeless, in which the class can participate? Are there shut-ins to visit? If your church already has sufficient help for those efforts, visit a nursing home and spend an afternoon with the elderly who are lonely.

Chapter 10: Mutual Edification

Chapter Summary

God has placed the saints in a position to grow in the faith and to help other believers grow, as well. This is the foundation and opportunity for mutual edification. The spiritual services that tend to mutual edification include both encouragement and correction. Since edifying one another exists for the glory of God, it is not voluntary; it is a spiritual necessity. Building up one another through encouragement and correction occurs among the saints in church worship, in small groups, in families, and in intimate friendships. Spiritual fellowship involves commitment, honesty, openness, and integrity. Wherever these virtues are present, the saints enter into deep and satisfying communion that promotes spiritual growth.

Objective

Your goal as class leader is to foster an appreciation for how believers are spiritually strengthened through the communion of saints.

Lesson

I. Open the class with a discussion of the following points from chapter 10:

1. Mutual edification involves encouragement and correction. Ask class members to name a specific time when they benefited spiritually from either encouragement or correction.
2. When we become aware of someone else's sin, what is the first thing we should do? What do we often tend to do instead?
3. What is necessary before correcting another believer? Why?
4. Why is offering correction often a frightening prospect?
5. How does encouragement differ from flattery?
6. In what contexts does mutual edification occur? Ask class members the specific contexts in which they give and receive spiritual edification. This class ought to be one example.
7. How does your church promote the gathering of small groups?

II. Study together the examples of mutual edification that follow:

1. The relationship between Elijah and Elisha, mentioned also in chapter 10, is covered in 1 and 2 Kings. For a small glimpse of the mutual edification that occurred through their relationship, ask someone to read aloud 2 Kings 2:1–15.
   a. In this brief passage, how was Elisha an encouragement to Elijah?
   b. How does Elisha benefit spiritually from his relationship with Elijah?
2. The apostle Paul and his protégé, Timothy, also had a spiritually enriching relationship. To get an idea of how they edified one another, look through Paul's letters to Timothy, focusing especially on 1 Timothy 1, 4, and 6; and on 2 Timothy 1 and 4. Discuss what you find.

Activity

Hebrews 10:24 commands us to consider how to spur one another on to love and good deeds. Challenge each member of the class to reach out in the week ahead with encouragement to a weary believer and with loving words of correction to an erring saint. Suggest that they engage in prayerful self-examination first, then pray for guidance and discernment before proceeding.

Chapter 11: All in the Family

Chapter Summary

Union with Christ overcomes racial, economic, and sexual divisions within the communion of saints. There are all kinds of differences between people groups, yet through union with Christ, they nevertheless hold everything in common. However, only in Christ are we reconciled both to God and to one another. When believers of varying gender, class, and race recognize both their equality in Christ and their complementarity, they are practicing the communion of saints.

Objective

Your goal as class leader is to demonstrate the need for and benefits of reconciliation within the body of Christ.

Lesson

I. Open discussion using the following questions:

1. Does your church foster racial reconciliation?
2. How does your church provide an environment in which the disabled can worship with the whole congregation?
3. What ministry roles are held by women in your congregation? Who are the recipients of their spiritual gifts?

II. The need for reconciliation is not something new in our era. Discrimination based on race, gender, and economic class has occurred throughout history. The Bible is full of examples of racial hatred and prejudice. Ask someone to read aloud Numbers 12:1–16. Then discuss the accompanying questions.

1. For what reason was Moses initially slandered in Numbers 12?
2. As Numbers 12 progresses, it becomes apparent that the discrimination was likely a cover-up for the jealousy that Miriam and Aaron felt toward Moses. What does that teach us about our fallen nature?
3. How did Miriam's punishment fit the crime?

III. Many mistakenly believe that reconciliation entails abolishing all ethnic, gender, and class distinctions. In reality, reconciliation occurs when we acknowledge and benefit from those distinctions. Continue the lesson with the following discussion questions:

1. How have you benefited from those in your church who come from a different walk of life? Consider race, financial circumstances, and those with disabilities.
2. How are the special cultural distinctions represented in your congregation brought out, rather than assimilated into the dominant culture?
3. Ask someone to read aloud Ephesians 5:22–33. Based on this passage, why is leadership distinction necessary in marriage?

Activity

Very likely there is a particular cultural group that makes up the majority of your congregation. If that is the case, speak to your pastor about holding a worship service exchange with another church. Invite members of a church made up of a different ethnic group to attend a

Sunday service in your church. Then plan another Sunday when the class, along with others from your church, will go to worship with their congregation.

Chapter 12: Worldwide Communion

Chapter Summary

Worldwide communion builds on what we studied in the last chapter about reconciliation within our homes and churches. Here we learn that a Christian can go anywhere in the world and immediately experience the love and embrace of brothers and sisters. Stronger than the bonds of blood relationships are the ties that bind one Christian to another. Involving ourselves with our brothers and sisters in Christ from all around the world is living out the communion of saints.

Objective

Your goal as class leader is to deepen class awareness of the existing unity of believers worldwide.

Lesson

I. The apostle Paul concluded most of his epistles by sending greetings to fellow Christians around the world. Begin the lesson on chapter 12 by looking together at the following passages from his epistles. Observe the specific ways Paul encouraged worldwide communion:

1. From Romans 16:3–16, discuss how those to whom Paul sends greetings have been a source of blessing to him.
2. In 1 Corinthians 16:19–23, what words of encouragement does Paul send to the saints in Corinth?
3. From Colossians 4:7–18, name all the ways you see worldwide communion practiced among the early believers. How do you

think these specific practices strengthened those early Christians?

II. We are all called to participate in the Great Commission in one way or another. Ask class members if they have sought God about their unique role. Is there anyone in class who has felt called to participate in the Great Commission by going overseas to live? What about other specific calls to go and make disciples? If so, how did they respond?

III. Come to class prepared with information about an overseas Christian or Christian missionary. Share with the group all you know about this particular brother or sister in Christ. Include where they live (if doing so doesn't endanger the missionary's safety), living conditions, troubles encountered, and victories achieved. Spend a few minutes praying specifically for this fellow saint. Then discuss practical ways to encourage him or her. Is this individual in need of some supplies that the class could readily accumulate and send? Ask the class to pray about specific ways that God may wish to use them in the life of this faraway believer. Perhaps it is writing a letter of encouragement or making a commitment to pray for him or her. Face-to-face fellowship may be impossible, but communion is not. You can practice worldwide communion by writing a group letter from the entire class, offering words of support. After each class member has signed the letter, ask for a volunteer to mail it during the upcoming week.

Activity

Investigate the possibility of linking up with a sister church as chapter 12 described. Begin by talking to your missions commission or the pastor in your church most closely tied to missions. They might have a church in mind already!

Chapter 13: For All the Saints

Chapter Summary

The communion of saints at its best will occur in heaven. In order for believers to enter into that heavenly communion, we must first be glorified. Glorification is the final step in our salvation, and it will occur at the same time that our bodies are resurrected. All the barriers set up against the full communion of saints here on earth will be broken down on that final day. That is heaven indeed! But the best thing about heaven is that God will be there. Our brightest hope is not being reunited with loved ones, as wonderful as that will be. It is rather communion with Christ.

Objective

Your goal as class leader is to help the group see the benefit of looking forward to the final and perfect communion of saints.

Lesson

I. The apostle Peter viewed this life as a journey toward our permanent home in heaven. He exhorted believers to see themselves as pilgrims who have not yet reached their permanent home but are pressing on to get there. Ask class participants to read aloud the following passages. Then discuss the accompanying questions:

1. Based on 1 Peter 1:3–7, what is our final inheritance like? Where is it now? How does cultivating a forward view toward the return of Christ help us in trials? Finally, how do present trials play into glorification?
2. From 1 Peter 1:13, how are we instructed to think about Christ's return?
3. Look at 1 Peter 2:11 and discuss how a heavenward focus can help us live godly lives now.

4. Based on Peter's words in 1 Peter 4:7, what view should we hold about the return of Jesus Christ?
5. From a careful look at 2 Peter 3:10–14, how does looking forward to the coming day of the Lord shape our conduct?

II. Chapter 13 explains that glorification is the final step in salvation. In a twinkling all believers will be instantly conformed to the image of Jesus Christ, because they will see him as he is. Look back through the chapter and talk about what you discovered about the process of glorification. Add to your discussion the following passages that mention that great and final step: Romans 8:28–30; 9:22–24; 2 Thessalonians 1:6–10; Hebrews 2:9–10.

III. Ask someone to read aloud Revelation 21:1–7. Discuss what this passage indicates is in store for all the saints.

Activity

The main thing that keeps us from having a pilgrim view like Peter's is our tie to the things of this life. Our relationships, our careers, our possessions all occupy our minds and hearts and keep our focus earthbound. Ask class members to prayerfully reflect over the week ahead on specific things that might be keeping them from focusing on heaven. Suggest that they list ways they will work to change the priority those things hold for them, in order to look not only forward, but more continually upward, as well.

Index of Scripture

Index of Names